AMERICAN IDEALS
CHARACTER AND LIFE

AMERICAN IDEALS CHARACTER AND LIFE

BY

HAMILTON WRIGHT MABIE

Framingham State College
Framingham, Massachusetts

Essay Index Reprint Series

 BOOKS FOR LIBRARIES PRESS
FREEPORT, NEW YORK

First Published 1913
Reprinted 1971

INTERNATIONAL STANDARD BOOK NUMBER:
0-8369-2240-9

LIBRARY OF CONGRESS CATALOG CARD NUMBER:
74-157965

PRINTED IN THE UNITED STATES OF AMERICA

CONTENTS

		PAGE
I.	CLEARING THE WAY	1
II.	DISCOVERY AND EXPLORATION	34
III.	POSSESSING THE CONTINENT	61
IV.	PROVINCIAL AMERICA IN LITERATURE	91
V.	SECTIONAL LITERATURE	128
VI.	NATIONAL LITERATURE	156
VII.	THE AMERICAN IN ART	189
VIII.	SCHOOL AND COLLEGE	214
IX.	UNIVERSITY AND RESEARCH WORK	245
X.	THE AMERICAN AND HIS GOVERNMENT	267
XI.	COUNTRY AND PEOPLE	295

AMERICAN IDEALS, CHARACTER AND LIFE

I

CLEARING THE WAY

For many years past Japan has held a first place in the interest of Americans, and they have followed its extraordinary and brilliant career, not only with admiration, but with an ardent desire to know the historical sources of a national strength directed with such intelligence and used with such efficiency. They were quick to perceive that a people does not suddenly appear on the stage of the world in command of such moral and physical forces unless it has been subjected to a severe discipline of spirit and mind, and they have been eager to discover the secret of modern Japan in the ideals and education of old Japan. This combination of subtle artistic instinct and skill with high military

AMERICAN IDEALS

efficiency; in what age-long training of eye, of imagination, of will, was it made possible? This inbred courtesy unimpaired by a swiftly acquired practical efficiency, this capacity for suddenly changing tools and weapons and yet using them with veteran ease and skill — the explanation of this vigor of the fiber of character and this facile intelligence lies deep in the history of old Japan; and there we have searched and fancied we have found it in the interpretations of a large group of native and foreign students and observers. And so there has been born in the hearts of intelligent Americans an admiration for the Japanese nation at once historical and prophetic; a deep respect for what has been accomplished, a keen anticipation of a career in the near and far future full of dramatic possibilities of achievement on the higher planes of civilization.

We have tried to understand Japan by gaining access to its fundamental ideas of life and character: those ideas of which its activities have been a varied but unified expression. It is my hope to make my own

CLEARING THE WAY

country in some small measure more comprehensible by definition of its historic ideas, its inheritance of religious, ethical and political convictions, the physical conditions under which it has been compelled to work out its vital problems and fashion its political institutions; to bring before you, so far as I am able, the American behind his political and business activities. This is no light task and is not approached in a light spirit. The long separation of the East and the West has made it difficult for the men of the East and the men of the West to understand one another; but I utterly reject the idea that they cannot understand one another; that differences of landscape, climate, religion, political and social ideal, have been so wrought into temperament and character that a permanent barrier has been built between the East and West. Such a barrier may exist for a little time in the minds of men of selfish interest and narrow racial feeling, but it has never risen in the minds of men of vision East or West; and the future belongs not to traders and race bigots, but to men who, in statesmanship and in commerce, recognize that the world, which has become a neighborhood, is on the way to become a brotherhood.

The German poet Goethe, one of the most penetrating thinkers and critics of the West, declared that the prime quality of the real critic is sympathy. There is no other approach to a man or a race. Men rarely understand that which they hate, but they rarely fail to understand that which they love. There was in the London of the time of Charles Lamb, that master of the essay of sentiment and humor, a man who was widely detested because he was of a peculiarly irritating dullness of mind. This man's name came up one day in conversation, and Lamb was asked if he did not hate him. "How can I hate a man I know?" was the illuminating answer of a writer who knew well the weaknesses of his fellows because he knew his own frailties. The French maxim, that to know all would be to forgive all, may need some qualification; but distrust, dislike and hatred are so often conceived in ignorance and born in blindness of mind that the truth at the heart of it may

CLEARING THE WAY

be safely accepted as a guide to judgment, and especially to international judgment. The beginning of wisdom in these matters is an open mind and the readiness to approach a nation along its own highways.

No man can understand a foreign people until he studies them in the light of their own ideals. France is a closed book to the Englishman or American who does not recognize at the start that in that country the social unit is the family, while among the English-speaking peoples the social unit is the individual. The French and English misunderstood one another for centuries, because they held stubbornly to certain preconceptions instead of approaching one another with open minds; and only lately, discarding old-time popular prejudgments, have they begun to recognize the great qualities which other peoples have seen in both nations. A nation of shopkeepers does not produce Tennysons, Darwins, Gladstones and Gordons; nor does a frivolous people given over to amusement, produce Gambettas, Pasteurs, Brunetières.

It has been the good fortune of Japan to

AMERICAN IDEALS

disarm many foreign critics at the very start and to lay a spell on many hard-minded but quick-spoken judges who would otherwise have been harsh judges of a people they approached with the preconceptions of the Western mind; but even Japan, most courteous of countries, has not escaped those who suspect everything that is strange and condemn everything they do not understand.

No people, however, have borne a heavier burden of misunderstanding than the Americans, and for very obvious reasons: differences of social structure and habit so radical and so fundamental that until they are taken into account the United States is, to the mind which approaches it from the European or the Oriental point of view, a vast and baffling confusion. From the very beginning there have been men and women who have gone to the Far West, as there have been those who have come to the Far East, not to judge, but to understand; and Americans are fortunate in possessing a small group of interpretations of their social and political life of classic quality. Between the hasty and ignorant

CLEARING THE WAY

and the open-minded and intelligent observers, the opinions expressed have been of such diversity that the American has reached a state of settled indifference toward average foreign opinion. He is told by one group of observers that his country is the home of materialism, that his people are crude, irreverent, indifferent to religion, to art, to culture; and he is told by another group that his is the land of religious enthusiasts; that he is a dreamer and a sentimentalist; that his supreme desire is not for money, but for education.

Intelligent criticism is a far greater evidence of friendship than indiscriminate praise, and neither the strong man nor the strong people should shrink from its occasional sting. Truth may weaken the weak; it strengthens the strong. In this matter of international understanding, which may turn out to be the chief business of this century, truth-speaking is of prime importance. But let it be remembered that the truth about a man or a nation is revealed to the sympathetic only; to all others there is and can be no revelation of racial spirit and character. "Over the gateway of the twentieth century," wrote the noble German thinker and teacher, Fichte, "shall be written the words: 'this is the way to virtue, to justice and to peace.'" And that these great ends may be reached and this century fulfill this inspiring prophecy, these other words of a Latin writer ought to be in the mind of every man who endeavors to interpret the life of a people: "neither to laugh nor to cry, but to understand."

During the dark days of the War between the States the North was astonished and bitterly disappointed by the attitude of many of the leaders of opinion in England. Forty years later in his Life of a great English statesman, Mr. Morley wrote: "Of this immense conflict Mr. Gladstone, like most leading statesmen of the time, and, like the majority of his own countrymen, failed to take the true measure. The error that lay at the root of our English misconceptions of the American struggle is now clear. We applied ordinary political maxims to what was not merely a political contest, but a social revolution."

CLEARING THE WAY

It is the habit of applying the ordinary political maxims of one country to the civilization of another country that has made a great deal of international comment like the game of blindman's buff played by children; in which there is much running to and fro, much noise and general confusion, ending in guessing more or less shrewd. A distinguished German student of American life describes one of his books as "a study of the Americans as the best of them are and the others should wish to be." Approached in this spirit, the student of a people may understate the seriousness of the external evils which afflict every state; he will almost unerringly discover the sources of its strength, and, above all, he will feel the throb of its vitality, which is the heartbeat of a nation.

And this is far and away the most important fact to learn about a people; for the ultimate question never is, "How many diseases has a nation?" The ultimate question always is, "How much vitality has it?" If it has a great store of vitality, its diseases are only episodes in its abundant life. It is easy to

AMERICAN IDEALS

enumerate the diseases from which a nation is suffering, for they are largely external, and this is the chief occupation of the majority of international observers; it requires insight, intelligence and sympathy to measure the vitality of a nation, and these qualities are lacking in the mass of observers, who are impressionists and whose opinions are colored, if not formed, by the superficial aspects of the life around them. There are perhaps half a dozen men in a generation in any country whose judgment on another country has value; there are many who are competent to report obvious conditions, to describe customs, to paint with charming skill the landscape which enfolds a nation's daily life; but there are only an elect few qualified by nature as well as by training to uncover the character — that is to say, the significant ideals, the organized energy, the sustaining vitality — of a foreign people, or to set in contrast the strength and weakness of two civilizations. The beginning of wisdom in this field is, without any surrender of convictions, to endeavor to understand and to

CLEARING THE WAY

postpone judgment to a time of fuller light, to escape entirely from racial prejudices and national preconceptions, to see with large intelligence behind the eyes, and to put away distrust and antipathy with the armor and weapons and tools that have been superseded by finer instruments.

It is easier to understand one's own country than to understand other countries, but it is no easy task to interpret a people one may know intimately to the people of another country. And this task becomes especially difficult when a Japanese endeavors to interpret his people to Americans or an American undertakes to reveal his people to the Japanese. But Japanese writers have succeeded in rendering this great service to Americans, and an American need not despair of conveying to the Japanese a definite if very inadequate conception of his own country. It may be that the breadth of contrast between the historical background of Japan and the United States gives to each country a definiteness of outline which would be lacking if one were attempting to contrast

AMERICAN IDEALS

the United States with any European country, and that the distance which has separated the paths by which we have come may give us a deeper and more open-minded interest in one another. In this hope I venture to sketch on a large canvas and with a free hand the spirit of the youngest of the leading nations to one of the oldest; a people spread over a continent to a people concentrated within island boundaries; a people organized around the individual as a unit, though lacking neither filial nor national loyalty, to a people in whom a profound and mystical conception of the family has bred a spirit of reverence and obedience, a love of kindred, of ruler and of country, which have armed the empire at the very heart; a people drawn from many countries and fed by many races to a people unified by ancient community of religion, of political ideals and of social order and custom.

If the chief end of civilization is to develop the genius of every race and to give every individual an opportunity of making his contribution to the welfare of the com-

CLEARING THE WAY

munity of races which the world is fast becoming, then the general movement which we call evolution will develop eventually, not uniformity of political and social conditions the world over, but the widest and richest diversities of political and social institutions, of educational method, of the forms of expression of the religious nature. And the full and cordial recognition of the variety and diversity of the aims and skills and methods of civilization is the measure of a man's understanding of the modern world.

To a man bred in another part of the world, the United States is a country of baffling confusion; he cannot understand its solidity and its apparent fluidity, its deep-rooted political convictions and its apparent indifference to political forms; its essential conservatism and the rapid growth of radical ideas in its atmosphere.

The differences between the political and social structure of the older countries and of this new country are manifold, but there are three or four which must be taken into

AMERICAN IDEALS

account at the very start if one is to get at the real character of the American people.

In a community organized on the basis of equality in political privilege and before the law, the influence of highly developed standards of speech and manners is not supreme; it is left to establish itself by the long process of popular education. There are as many men and women of thorough education and ripeness of mind in the United States as in any other country, but they are not organized into a class, and they have never defined the standards of speech and manners. Whenever they have attempted to do this, a jealous democracy, entirely lacking in reverence for class distinctions, has overwhelmed them with ridicule. For superior education, for ability of a high order, for the finer aspects of character, there is great respect in the American community; but for any arrogation of social superiority, there is swift and contemptuous indignation. Of the twenty-seven Presidents of the United States, nineteen have been men of university training; but three Presidents who have

CLEARING THE WAY

lacked this training — Washington, Lincoln and Cleveland — have been statesmen and patriots whose conspicuous service to the Commonwealth has evidenced the educational influence which issues from the institutions and spirit of the country. Washington and Lincoln, born at the two extremes of society so far as social conditions are concerned, must be classed with Franklin and Emerson, among the most representative products of the popular education which is perhaps the most important function of the American system. In the election for President recently held in the United States there were three candidates for that high office; of these one was a member of the governing body of Yale University; another, after graduation from Princeton University and further study at the Johns Hopkins University, for ten years previous to his election as Governor of his State, had been president of Princeton University; while the third is a member of the Board of Overseers of Harvard University, the oldest of American institutions of the higher rank, and is a man of notable intel-

AMERICAN IDEALS

lectual achievements and accomplishments. Two of these gentlemen are historians and authors of distinction. From the beginning, public life in the United States has been crowded with men of university education; the respect for education has deepened into a faith so intense that it has become almost a superstition, and both public and private funds flow with a kind of tidal movement to the support of education and the enrichment of its institutions.

Nevertheless, the man whose schooling, like Lincoln's, has been "less than a year" and who has never crossed the threshold of a university, has no more consciousness of inferiority in the presence of the president of the oldest university than the lawyer has in the presence of the physician, or the architect in the presence of the engineer. He recognizes cordially that another is better equipped than he in a special kind of work, but as a man he has not the slightest sense of inequality. He knows that the doors of opportunity are open to him and that he can go as far as his ability and energy will carry him.

CLEARING THE WAY

Americans believe profoundly in the system which rests the government on the broadest foundation of suffrage, which makes all men partners in the national enterprise, which exacts no special preparation of the man who takes part in public affairs, but holds the doors wide, so that a man may start at the bottom of the social order and go to the top. They believe in it, not because they think it has always secured for them the most economical or efficient government; but because they believe it the most just and, in the long run, the safest form of political organization; and because they believe it gives the processes of government a fundamental educational value which has made the country a vast school for the education of people of all classes in that political character of which political institutions are the vital expression. For the strength of a people issues from the political character behind their institutions, and the institutions are real and vital only in so far as they express that character. This is what Hamilton, one of the four or five men who had most to do with framing the Ameri-

AMERICAN IDEALS

can Constitution and creating its government, had in mind when he wrote: "The truth is that the general genius of a government is all that can be substantially relied upon for permanent effects. Particular provisions, though not altogether useless, have far less virtue and efficiency than are commonly ascribed to them; and the want of them will never be, with men of sound discernment, a decisive objection to any plan which exhibits the leading characters of a good government."

This is not equivalent to saying that all forms of government have equal value; it is equivalent to saying that a self-controlled and disciplined people will give a good account of themselves in spite of defective political institutions. The general genius of a government is the genius of a people organized into institutions and embodied in laws. The searching discipline which in the life of old Japan laid the foundations of modern Japan, and explains its efficiency, could not have been enforced if it had not conformed to the genius of the people.

CLEARING THE WAY

Americans believe that, under widely different conditions, they have developed the love of country and the desire to serve the nation with the fullest consecration of individual gifts, which give Japan organized strength and skill.

But they are not blind to the perils of this system, nor are they unconscious of the difficulties which it presents to men of older communities who sincerely endeavor to understand it. Such observers find it difficult to believe that the order and self-control, which are the primary conditions of government, can be secured in communities in which individuality has such freedom of expression and of action that it seems at times to obscure and threaten the very existence of the state. Above all, they are confused by the absence of authoritative sources of public opinion, by the diversity of sentiment on all manner of questions which affect the public welfare, which, at times, gives the country the appearance of a vast debating society instead of a stable, strongly organized community. They hear a noisy confusion of

AMERICAN IDEALS

sounds when they look for an authoritative expression of national judgment; they find uneducated and unthinking people confidently and noisily asserting their representative capacity as Americans; they find the American press conspicuously displaying the disorders of the country in headlines that seem by their very size to indicate the immense significance of the crimes, scandals and violations of law which they report. "Democracy," said Pasteur, "is that order in the state which permits each individual to put forth his utmost effort." The American believes so completely in this system, so far as his own country is concerned, that he is willing to accept the excesses of individuality which are inseparable from it.

But he is not blind to the risks of misrepresentation to which the country is exposed. He is not disturbed by these excesses because he sees them in perspective; the foreign observer, unfortunately, sees them out of perspective. There are people of vulgar speech, manners and dress in every country; people of this type are no more

CLEARING THE WAY

numerous in America than in other countries, and they have qualities which are often lacking in the vulgarians of other nationalities. They are usually disposed to be helpful and neighborly; they feel themselves responsible for the comfort of women and the safety of children. But they have, as a rule, larger means than people of the same type in other countries, and they are more given to travel. They spend more lavishly than the same class in other countries, and they are more given to self-assertion. As a result they convey the impression that the vulgarian exists in far greater numbers in America than elsewhere. As a matter of fact, he does not; but, lacking the repression which recognized authority, either legal or social, imposes upon people of his type under other systems, he is much more in evidence. His assumption of equality, which is a matter of course at home, often becomes aggressive and offensive abroad; and his patriotism, which finds ready and normal expression in his own community, is heightened abroad into a kind of flamboyant Americanism which is often a

AMERICAN IDEALS

childish expression of love of country rather than an intention to affront the people whose guest he happens to be. Japan is the only country in the world in which politeness has been made part of the national discipline; in all other countries it is a matter of social tradition and standards, of family training or of individual instinct and cultivation. The American vulgarian traveling abroad is so vociferous that he multiplies himself; and becomes, to those who cannot see him in perspective, representative of a host of people in his own land, when, as a matter of fact, he stands for no larger minority than the vulgarian in other countries.

Americans have always traveled in large numbers, and Europe and the Far East have furnished the opportunities and the materials for a kind of popular university course for many whose means have outstripped their education, and the fact that they sometimes misrepresent the country from which they come is a small price to pay for the gains they make in knowledge and breadth of view through contact with other types of civiliza-

CLEARING THE WAY

tions and with the art and genius of the older world.

In the open field of individual endeavor, training comes largely through practice, and Americans not only pay great sums of money for popular education, but make great sacrifices of time, patience and of good repute among other nations by permitting preparation for every kind of public work to be made in public rather than in the privacy of the schools. This is one of the most radical aspects of democracy and one which is most disconcerting to men bred under other systems. To such men it seems incredible that a man without special training should reach the great position of the Presidency; an office not only of great honor, but clothed with powers transcending those intrusted to heads of state in many less democratic governments. The question of the possibility of wisely directing the affairs of a vast community without technical training has been answered in America many times by the appearance in the forefront of public affairs of men of great capacity and dignity of character, who have shown special aptitude for dealing wisely and strongly with questions of national policy. As a matter of fact, none of these men of light and leading has lacked education for his work, but the education has not been academic. Lincoln had a preparation, that is to say, an education, for his immense responsibilities that could hardly have been more completely fitted to his needs if he had passed through every grade of school and college. Side by side with their passionate faith in formal education, Americans have a deep and unshakable faith in the educational influence of their ideals of life organized in their institutions, in the large liberty of action which they enjoy, in the inspiration of hope and the stimulation of individual initiative, which are in the air they breathe. Their system rests on faith in the capacity of men to govern themselves by intrusting them with full responsibility for the management of the greatest affairs of society; and they believe that whatever mistakes may be made by the way, — and they have been many and serious, — the state gains in the long run the

CLEARING THE WAY

service of men who have learned in the school of national life how, wisely and effectively, to give expression to that life.

The standards of requirement for the professions and for all occupations in America are now practically what they are in older countries; the quality of the training in the American military and naval academies is well understood in Japan; the movement towards more exacting requirements in all departments of the government service goes steadily forward; nevertheless, it remains true that access to the public in America is open to every one who is sufficiently eager or ambitious to secure the means. The result is a large and often clamorous expression of ill-digested opinions, which range from the naïve simplicity of childlike ignorance to the most fantastic radicalism. There is probably no theory of religion, no conception of government, no ideal of social life, that has not been exploited in America; and often by those whose perfectly obvious ignorance of elementary facts have shown them, at the very start, entirely without the capacity

AMERICAN IDEALS

for public teaching. In Europe, as a rule, access to the public through books, magazines, addresses, sermons, pamphlets, is secured only by those who have some educational qualifications for the responsibility they have taken upon themselves. The views expressed may be subversive of every existing institution, — for there is far more radicalism of a destructive kind in Europe than in the United States, — but the man who speaks or writes, as a rule, brings to his work some degree of intellectual preparation and commands, therefore, a certain degree of attention.

In America, on the other hand, any man may write or speak who can secure the use of a platform or command the services of a printer. There is, as a result, a vast amount of talking and of writing which is of no importance to any one but the speaker or writer, and which greatly confuses the observer who is trying to ascertain the drift of public opinion. In the great public school which the American community has become, the various grades make their recitations with equal emphasis, and the man of another country

CLEARING THE WAY

finds it difficult to distinguish between those who are just beginning to learn the rudiments of knowledge and those who have become expert. In this respect America is a noisy and confusing country in which, at times, every one seems to be talking at once; and those who have the least claim on public attention are often the most vociferous.

It happens, therefore, when an international question arises, that those who know least about it become voluble and clamorous and seem at the moment to express the convictions of a nation, when, as a matter of fact, their talk is like the foam on a sea which is restless only at its edges. In all countries there is a class of men who are made giddy by international questions and rush into declamation before the country has begun to think. Of men of this temper in public life, America has perhaps more than its share, — though it must be remembered that the most thorough training often fails to put reason in command of emotion in moments of tense feeling; and these unseasoned talkers and writers sometimes assume to speak for the

AMERICAN IDEALS

nation when the nation does not give them a passing thought. America is often grossly misrepresented by these ardent but unintelligent orators, whose utterances are endured at home as part of the price of popular government, but are taken abroad as serious expressions of national opinion. In spite of the ear-piercing noise of escaping steam, Americans believe in keeping the throttle valves open and enduring the discomfort for the sake of the safety.

This same latitude of expression makes the American press a powerful organ of healthful opinion on the one hand, and a serious menace to the higher life of the country on the other. Journalism is one of the latest occupations to secure the rank of a profession; under the American system it is as great a necessity as the transcontinental railways. All public questions ultimately reach the people and are settled by them; they constitute, therefore, a great jury to whom, in all debated matters, the evidence must be submitted. The newspaper is the medium through which facts and arguments are presented to the jury. In many respects this duty — for such it is to a man who has any sense of responsibility for the use of a powerful instrument for good or evil — is discharged with ability and intelligence. For the newspaper has passed through the preliminary stage of purely individualistic enterprise and, in many cases, has taken on something approaching institutional stability and continuity. The age of the newspaper created and directed by one strong man of marked individuality who made his journal a personal organ has passed; a first-class newspaper of to-day is a highly organized enterprise conducted by a group of men, the majority of whom are often men of university training.

But while journalism as a whole has passed through this evolution, a new and lower type of newspaper has come into existence, the special characteristic of which is the gathering of news of all sorts and kinds and its presentation in the most sensational form. The collection of news has been raised to the dignity of a science by the American press, in the service of which able men have shown the

AMERICAN IDEALS

highest qualities of daring, devotion, self-denial, self-sacrifice and dauntless energy. In journals of the higher class, readers are kept in close touch with the current history of the world in all fields of endeavor; in journals of the lower class the emphasis is laid on whatever is sensational in eccentricity, criminality or social offensiveness. The competition for news is so keen that nothing escapes to which any degree of interest attaches. Morning and evening, the entire continent is swept clean of every fact, rumor or report that can furnish material for a headline. No event is so local or so trivial as to escape the notice of these news scavengers; for such this class of reporters are. No place, time or person is sacred to them; no pity for sorrow, no regard for the innocent, no consideration for the unfortunate, no sense of justice, halts for a moment this relentless search for anything that can, by any heightening or lowering of the lights, any perversion of facts, any use of insinuation or suggestion, gain a scandalous interest. I speak only of the sensational newspaper, but there are so

CLEARING THE WAY

many newspapers of this type that they constitute a real menace to the higher life of the nation, and they must be taken into account in any attempt to understand the America of To-day. These journals have made the discovery that uneducated men and women are interested primarily in the personal aspects of news, and their endeavor is to report news about persons with the ruthless detail of the most radical realist. And, in order to give it dramatic interest, they stop at no perversion or exaggeration. The foreign reader of American newspapers is appalled by the number and variety of legal, moral and social offenses reported — murders, outbreaks of mob violence, crimes against property and against the family, shameful, or, rather, shameless, divorces, eccentricities, vulgarities, frivolities so insignificant that they lie below the normal interest of a country journal. Such a reader wonders how a country so given over to crime and folly can live for a day and does not know that he is reading on one page all the crimes and peccadillos he would discover if he read all the local journals in his own country. In some newspapers village gossip has assumed national proportions and importance.

If the foreign observer is not to be as grossly misled with regard to moral and social conditions as he has been too often with regard to the attitude of Americans toward money, he must take into account the excess of publicity in America. It is not too much to say that there is five times as much publicity in America as in England, ten times as much as in Germany, twenty times as much as in Russia, and fifty times as much as in India. He must make large allowance also for perversions, exaggerations and inventions so ingenious, so daring and often so original, that they reveal misdirected capacity for fiction writing. He must remember that in journals of the sensational kind the endeavor is not to present facts, but to tell a thrilling or dramatic story.

To understand Japan, an American must free his mind of many preconceptions; to understand America, the Japanese student must not only free his mind of his precon-

CLEARING THE WAY

ceptions of political and social order, but must learn how little real importance in America many persons have who seem to speak with authority; how misleading the utterances of public men often are unless one knows their character and standing; and how grossly many American newspapers misrepresent the spirit of the nation and the daily life of the people.

II

DISCOVERY AND EXPLORATION

THE fortunes of the Far West have been interwoven with those of the Far East from the first discoveries. The peoples who traveled farthest from the plains of Asia lost touch with those who stayed nearer the earliest home of the race, but were never wholly severed from them. The separation of the different races in Europe during the Middle Ages was almost as great as the separation between Europe and Asia. After the final collapse of the Roman Empire, which made way for the development of modern nationalities, war was the chief form of intercourse between the rising communities that were becoming nations. At the close of that period the two centuries in which the crusaders stirred the imagination of Europe and disturbed the peace of the nearer Orient renewed an acquaintance which had become fitful and occasional, spread curiosity about

DISCOVERY AND EXPLORATION

Oriental life, and made Europe aware of the art and luxury of the Far East. Trade between the two sections began to grow; for, while Europe had only metals, woolens and minerals to sell, it was an eager purchaser of spices, cinnamon, pepper, ginger, of precious stones from India and Persia, of pearls from Ceylon, of drugs, perfumes and sweet-smelling woods from Borneo and Sumatra, of glass from Damascus and Samarcand, of porcelain from China, of silk, satins, tapestries, rugs from Cashmere and from half a hundred ancient cities. Oriental merchants became familiar figures in the Mediterranean ports, and the traffic in fragrant and beautiful things not only grew into an organized commerce, but gave the relations between East and West an element of romantic interest. Centuries later, when the ships built in the shipyards of New England made their long voyages to India and China, the boys who spent their half holidays on the old docks came to associate the Far East with the penetrating fragrance which was wafted ashore from hidden cargoes.

AMERICAN IDEALS

The commerce between Europe and Asia was in the last degree adventurous and perilous, but it developed into an extensive trade carried on along three routes. The southernmost, following the coast from Japan through the Malay Islands, touched at Ceylon, passed up the Arabian Sea and through the Persian Gulf to Persia; or, crossing the Arabian Sea, reached Cairo and the Mediterranean by way of the Red Sea. This was an all-sea route, and, though beset with perils, was less dangerous and fatiguing than the more northern routes. Of these there were two. One started on the eastern coast of China, crossed that country to Turkestan, and, by means of a network of shorter routes, opened up the cities of Persia, of Palestine, of Asia Minor, and brought eastern Europe and western Asia into contact on the Bosporus and the Black Sea. The other and northernmost route started from Peking, crossed China on its northern boundaries, and by way of Kashgar, Bakhara and the shores of the Aral and Caspian seas, crossed the Volga and reached the Black Sea. These main lines of

DISCOVERY AND EXPLORATION

transportation were connected by short routes with the centers of European trade; from the terminals on the Mediterranean goods from the Orient were carried by water to Pisa, Venice, Genoa, Barcelona, Marseilles, London and other English ports, and to Belgium; whence they were sent by land to Germany, France and the Netherlands.

For many decades, by caravans of camels, on the backs of mules, or of stout carriers capable of almost incredible feats of strength in walking long distances with heavy loads, by seacraft and river boats of many shapes, the Far East traded with the West, and at the beginning of the fifteenth century European merchants had their quarters in many Eastern cities; and communication between East and West, though perilous, was well established and fairly regular.

Then the Turks appeared on the scene, and the control of the Eastern Mediterranean passed into their hands. The fall of Constantinople in 1453 was followed by the conquest of the territories held by Venice, of the islands of the Greek archipelago, of Lesbos

AMERICAN IDEALS

and Chios, long under the rule of Genoa. Turkish fleets preyed on trading ships along the Levant, while the northern routes were disturbed by recurring wars. For a time goods from Asia were sent through the ports on the Red Sea and through Syria, but early in the sixteenth century this great territory fell into Turkish hands.

Few events have so rapidly made radical changes in the economic conditions of the world as the appearance of the Turks in Europe. The Italian cities, which had been the distributing centers of the old commerce, declined; commercial supremacy passed from Venice to Amsterdam; trade between the East and the West was blocked, and the discovery of America became inevitable in the near future.

Many influences were at work which would sooner or later have brought the New World above the western horizon, but the barriers between East and West made it necessary to establish new routes of communication. Europe was rapidly increasing in wealth, the luxuries supplied by the East were increasingly

DISCOVERY AND EXPLORATION

valued; and the love of beauty, stimulated by the Renaissance, craved the art of the East. To find a new passage to the Orient became the dream of the adventurous navigators of Italy, Portugal, Spain and England. Italian mathematicians' maps, charts, ships and sailors were ready, and when Italian commercial prosperity began to wane, Italian influence through the arts, through literature and science, rendered the world services of incalculable value. Italy played no such part in the actual discovery of America as Spain, Portugal, France and England; but she was the teacher of all these nations in the art of navigation, and she was the maker of their instruments. When the commerce of the East was taken out of her hands, she turned the mind of Europe westward and led the way to that enlargement of the world which has made East and West members of the community of nations.

The fact that America was discovered in the endeavor to find a new way of getting to the East, and that the newest world was brought into view incidentally by men on their way to the oldest world, is a striking evidence of an interrelation of races which neither ignorance nor selfishness can defeat; for the ends of the earth are bound together by conditions which have the force of laws of nature. When Columbus sailed from Palos in August, 1492, his object was to reach the Indies; and on his last voyage, six years later, he was under the illusion that the eastern coast of South America was the western coast of Asia. He died in ignorance of the fact that he had discovered a continent. When John Cabot was wrecked on the rocky shores of Labrador in 1496, he was on his way to Japan and the countries from which caravans brought goods to Alexandria; and in taking formal possession of the country he believed that he was extending the rule of the English king, Henry VII, into Asia. Europe was obsessed, so to speak, with the conviction that there was a western passage to the East, and to the commercial necessity of such a passage was added the allurement of Eastern wealth and splendor in China, Japan and India, reported by Marco Polo and his brother, the daring Venetian travelers.

DISCOVERY AND EXPLORATION

Cipango, as Japan was known in those and later days, was described as abounding in "gold, pearls and precious stones," its "temples and palaces covered with gold." Columbus called the inhabitants of the island in the group of the Bahamas on which he first landed, Indians, because he supposed he had found India; and he was convinced, first that Cuba, and later, Hayti, was the island of Cipango. So deeply rooted was the conviction that Asia had been reached across the western sea that the great discoverers and explorers of Columbus' day never knew that they had enlarged the world by a hemisphere; and Amerigo Vespucci died in ignorance of the fact that his name was to be added to the list of names of continents.

It was not until 1541, half a century after the discovery, that the New World appeared on Mercator's map distinct and separate from Asia, and the first feeling which dominated Europe when the real significance of the discoveries in the West dawned on the Old World was poignant regret that the new lands interposed another obstacle between the

AMERICAN IDEALS

West and the East. These facts are dramatically significant in these days when Japan and the United States have become neighbors, and the Pacific Ocean is likely to become as familiar a highway between nations as the Atlantic has long been.

When the illusion that West was East and the New World part of the oldest world was dissipated, the mind of Europe was still under the spell of dreams of wealth to be found in the lands beyond seas. Stories of the treasures which the Spaniards had discovered in Mexico and Peru invested the entire Atlantic coast with irresistible interest for adventurers, gentlemen of fallen fortunes, and young men of restless ambition in England; and the first English settlement in the country which is now the United States, at Jamestown, in Virginia, in 1607, was made by men who were in search of gold or of an open way to the Pacific Ocean. From these dreams the colonists awoke to the hard conditions of pioneers in a new world; and, with the practical genius of their race, they began to raise tobacco; they established local government;

DISCOVERY AND EXPLORATION

they discovered the value of the negroes brought to them by a Dutch ship in 1619, and slave labor found its earliest lodgment in American soil. At the start the new countries were a refuge from oppressive conditions in Europe, and the early colonies were primarily doors of escape from various forms of oppressive interference with religious faith, political conviction or individual activity.

The triumph of the Puritan party in England and the establishment of the Commonwealth sent to Virginia, between 1640 and 1660, a small army of men and women who were loyal to the monarchy, many of whom were of the Cavalier class. On the stones which mark the graves in the ancient churchyard in Williamsburgh, many old English titles are recorded. These emigrants had been landholders at home, and they became owners of great plantations in Virginia, and brought the habits of English country life into the wilderness. They were men of aristocratic temper; they became masters of vast tracts of land cultivated by slave labor; they brought the Established Church of

AMERICAN IDEALS

England with them, and made the parish the unit of local government. Men of this class, isolated from one another and managing large estates, developed unusual abilities as organizers and leaders, and when the colonists threw off allegiance to the British Crown, they furnished many of the foremost leaders of the movement. From this class came Washington, Madison, Marshall.

The second settlement of Englishmen in North America was made at Plymouth in 1620 by the Pilgrims; the Puritans came eight years later and settled on the same coast fifty miles to the north. There were temperamental differences between these two groups of settlers of the New England colonists, but they shared certain fundamental convictions, they were impelled by the same motives, and were soon blended in a common endeavor to establish a new order of society in the New World. The withdrawal of the English Church from the communion of the Roman Catholic Church was partly political and partly religious. It was an assertion of the political as well as the religious independence

DISCOVERY AND EXPLORATION

of England from foreign authority. It began with a denial of the supremacy of the Pope; it ended with a rejection of his title to the headship of the Christian Church and the rejection of many of the doctrines, practices and rites which had come into the Church since the establishment of the Papacy. But this reassertion of the authority of the English Church against the claims of the Church of Rome did not end with the recovery of religious independence; it became a powerful movement for the liberation of the English mind. It did not stop short of a searching inquiry into the nature of authority in matters of religious belief, into the soundness of the statements of faith, into the forms of worship.

The decrees of the councils of the church, long accepted without question, and the formularies of theology which had become, not statements of faith, but its foundations, were subjected to free and rigid scrutiny. A marvelously fresh and inspiring translation of the Bible put into the hands of the English people the text of a book of which they had received only authoritative interpretations, and they were in a position to ask and answer for themselves questions which went to the very foundations of the claims of ecclesiastical authority and of the creeds. The Bible had, moreover, this great and distinguishing quality among books which claim to be revelations of the Divine nature: it was not a body of principles, maxims and regulations; it was a revelation in terms of history; it was not a philosophical solution of the problems of life, but a disclosure of the nature of the power behind the universe as that nature was expressed in the experience of the race. It affirmed the authority of certain moral laws, and it showed how those laws had been enforced in the experience of many hundred years. And this story of the Divine unveiling itself in the souls of men and in the events of history culminated in the biography of a Teacher whose supreme power resided neither in maxims nor in deeds, but in a nature of such divine purity and of such love for, and sympathy with, humanity that He spoke with the authority of the truth itself.

DISCOVERY AND EXPLORATION

This noble literature — sixty-six books of history, biography, prophecy, poetry, moral teaching, religious aspiration, bound between the covers of a single volume — spoke to the awakened mind and heart of the English, not only with the authority of religion, but with the power of great literature. The liberating energy of a book charged with vitality went out of it into the imagination and conscience, and it became and remains the most powerful influence in the civilization of the English speaking peoples.

The separation of the English from the Roman Church was inevitably followed by a sharp division of parties within the English Church. There were those who held that the supremacy of the Pope having been rejected, the traditions, the practices and the faith of the Roman Church should be preserved; and there were those who insisted on a radical revision of doctrine and of ritual, and that the simplicity of the apostolic age should be restored. The mind of the nation was deeply stirred; debate grew more acrimonious; differences of point of view became more radical; the attempt to compel uniformity of worship failed; the Protestant party became more aggressive; oppressive measures were adopted with the usual results. As time went on, the differences became irreconcilable.

The Puritans, as the radical reformers came to be called, protested not only against the mass and the authority of the priest, but against vestments, ritual, written prayers, altars, saints' days, the observance of Christmas. It was a struggle to the death, for the idea of religious toleration did not occur to either party; the alternative to establishment of one's convictions was their total abandonment. The declaration of national independence in religion ended in the banishment or withdrawal of a large number of Puritans, the civil war and the downfall of the Stuart dynasty, the founding of powerful colonies beyond the sea, and contributed largely to the impulses which brought on the American Revolution.

Puritanism went far before it exhausted itself. It set itself against all authority in

DISCOVERY AND EXPLORATION

religion except the Bible interpreted by the individual conscience, against the conception of the Church as having any authority beyond that of voluntary organization, against the priest as clothed with any greater power than that of a religious teacher specially set apart to the work of teaching. It revolted against forms of all kinds, although it inevitably developed a form of its own; it rejected art and laid its ban on beauty; and it finally attempted to organize a society on a religious basis, in which only people who subscribed to the Puritan creed could exercise the rights of citizenship. It became in the end the most radical expression of extreme individualism.

But with many limitations of vision and much hardness of heart it had deep sources of strength. It insisted on purity of life and laid unescapable and invigorating emphasis on character; it asserted the supremacy of the law in private and public life; it taught the reality of a man's direct responsibility to God and the authority of the individual conscience; it held education in great respect, and many of its leaders were men of university training; it made the Bible the textbook of English civilization; it made men strong because they believed the divine power was behind them; self-denying and indifferent to hardship because they believed in the supreme value of things of the spirit. It made them sober in life, tireless in industry, and of a sturdy independence of spirit. Notwithstanding its narrowness and intolerance in religion and its rigidity of life, the spirit of Puritanism was the spirit of freedom, and both in England and in America it was a mighty force in the struggle for liberty. No study of American society is intelligent without some understanding of the Puritan movement and spirit. As the head of one of the foremost American universities, Dr. Nicholas Murray Butler, has said: "Puritanism built New England, and for nearly a hundred years New England powerfully influenced the United States. . . . The fact must not be overlooked that New England Puritanism, built on the rock of Geneva, is the secure theological and philosophical foundation on

DISCOVERY AND EXPLORATION

which all that is distinctive in American life and culture has been built. . . . This fact explains much of the narrowness and lack of sympathy with strange customs and views which one observes among Americans, and it explains also much of the determination and energy of the American temperament. Devotion to duty for its own sake, and a determination to persevere to the end in any undertaking simply because it has been undertaken, are almost universal American applications of Calvinism."

The Pilgrims, driven into exile, found a refuge in Holland; a little country with a passion for liberty, and hospitable to men who were persecuted for their religious opinions. The struggle through which the Dutch had passed in defense of their country and of their faith had not only developed a splendid vigor of character in them, but had given them a sense of leadership in the fight for religious freedom in which western Europe was deeply concerned.

The Dutch were also daring adventurers, traders and far-seeing merchants, and it fell

AMERICAN IDEALS

to them to found the commercial metropolis of the New World and to make a notable contribution to its citizenship and ideals. In 1609, two years after the founding of the Virginia colony, Henry Hudson, an Englishman in the service of the Dutch East India Company, who had made two attempts to reach Asia by the way of the Polar Sea, sailed up the river which now bears his name in the endeavor to find the elusive Northwest Passage, and was disappointed to discover that it was not a waterway to the Far East. Fourteen years later, in 1623, a Dutch colony was planted on the island which has long been known as the city of New York. The colonists were sturdy men, with a genius for trade; they bought the island from the Indians for about one hundred and twenty-five dollars, and were soon engaged in a profitable business in buying furs and selling them in Europe. The great trading companies which not only broadened the area of commerce in the sixteenth and seventeenth centuries, but were intrusted with governmental powers, had much to do with the early settlement of

DISCOVERY AND EXPLORATION

America, and were especially influential in the Dutch colonies on the Hudson River. A monopoly of trade in these colonies was granted to the New Netherland Company, which was speedily succeeded by the much more ambitious West India Company, which was clothed with almost sovereign powers. It named all the public officers and could remove them, administered justice, built forts, made treaties, and was required to build and keep a small fleet of war vessels in commission.

England and Holland had a common foe during the early period of exploration and colonization. Both had gone through life-and-death struggles with Spain; which, until her defeat by the two rising Protestant nations, had been the foremost Power in Europe. The enormous revenues which Spain received from her colonies in Central and South America had supplied her with means to carry on the struggle against England and Holland, and after her efforts to subjugate both countries had been defeated, the war was transferred to the other side of the Atlantic and became a struggle for supremacy in the

AMERICAN IDEALS

New World. The founding of colonies was therefore, so far as these governments were concerned, not only a commercial enterprise, but a war measure. It is interesting to remember that the fight to keep the control of the New World out of Spanish hands, begun in the sixteenth century, did not reach its ultimate conclusion until the retirement of the Spanish from Cuba in 1898.

A fort was constructed on the water front of the island of Manhattan, a modification of the Indian name, a row of log houses built, and two hundred immigrants became the forerunners of the Greater New York of to-day, with a population of over four millions. Trade prospered, great estates were created under a system of landholding which was essentially feudal; but the political affairs of the colony were not well managed, and in 1664 it passed under English control.

One of the main streams of French immigration reached New York and contributed very attractive qualities to its social life. The Huguenots, the Protestants of France, although sorely persecuted and finally exiled,

DISCOVERY AND EXPLORATION

did not lose those qualities which have developed in France what Matthew Arnold happily called "the power of social life." They were men and women of deep-seated conviction and dauntless courage, but they never lost their aptitude for the amenities of life.

The Pennsylvania colony, which was neighbor on the south to the Dutch colony, was founded in 1682 by William Penn and the group of people who called themselves Friends, and were called derisively Quakers. Their characteristics were simplicity of dress and speech, absolute toleration of opinion, and faith in the equality of all men and women before the law. The root both of their faith and practice was the belief that in every human soul the Divine Spirit is present and gives direct inspiration and guidance. This illumination they called the Inner Light. They were persecuted both in England and in New England, and in weak or unbalanced minds their faith naturally took radical and sometimes fantastic forms of expression; but they were a high-minded people, who hated war and slavery. Their leader was one of the most influential men in the early history of the country, and the city which bears his name was one of the centers of intellectual and educational influence from the beginning. The government was paternal, peace was made and kept with the Indians, and the proprietary system with Penn as lord proprietor worked well throughout the colonial period. The liberal policy of Penn secured a rapid increase in the number of colonists, and attracted not only people of English birth, but the vigorous and hardy Scotch-Irish, the Dutch, the French and the Swedes.

Maryland, which lies next south of Pennsylvania, was also organized under a proprietary government,— a form of government which survived from feudal times in England, under which the overlord was a kind of viceroy and was clothed with almost regal powers. In this way Maryland was ruled for sixty years by successive Lords Baltimore, who, although Roman Catholics, pursued a policy of such liberality that the colony was for a time the refuge of people of widely different creeds. It was, however, too early

DISCOVERY AND EXPLORATION

in the education of the colonists to maintain this large and wise freedom, and the later history of Maryland as a colony was marred by bitter strife for supremacy among the different faiths.

To the south of Virginia lay the two Carolinas. The first settlement made in North Carolina was by a company of Virginians; a little later a group of English planters from the Barbadoes cast in their fortunes with the colony. A plan of government said to have been devised by the English philosopher, John Locke, was tried in North Carolina; but the settlers, who were of a vigorous, independent temper, refused to accept it, and it was abandoned. In later years the population contained large accessions of Germans and Scotch-Irish. The conditions of life in the colony long remained those of the frontier; there were no cities; the farmers and woodmen who laid the foundations of the future towns were men of great independence of spirit, impatient of restraint, lovers of the wilderness; a hardy, manly people who hated taxes and desired only to be let alone.

AMERICAN IDEALS

The early population of South Carolina was also English, but the revocation of the Edict of Nantes by Louis XIV in 1685 sent a large emigration of Huguenots to this colony; a people of heroic temper, of whom it has been said that they "had the virtues of the English Puritans without their bigotry."

Colonial history in America closed with the first movement of emigration from the seaboard at the close of the War for Independence. The thirteen colonies which faced the Atlantic from New England to the Carolinas were settled by men of English, Dutch, French, blood; with a mixture of Scotch-Irish, German and Swedish blood, — vigorous races who sent their most vigorous, independent and adventurous representatives to face the perils and master the difficulties of the exploration and settlement of a new world. They were drawn to that world by three or four of the major motives which stir men to undertake new enterprises and to risk the "hazards of new fortune." The earliest discoverers were one and all seekers after a westward way to the Far East, and they died

DISCOVERY AND EXPLORATION

in the belief that they had found the eastern shores of Asia. This misapprehension hung over the mind of Europe for several decades; when it disappeared it was succeeded by other illusions, — that the seaboard rivers ran to the westward sea and so made navigation to India, Japan and China possible; that the new countries were full of cities of vast wealth and the country of inexhaustible mines; that there were streams in the Far West in which, if a man bathed, his vanished youth returned.

These delusions were cherished chiefly by the Spanish explorers and settlers; the men and women who founded the English colonies had confused ideas of the conditions they were to face, but were urged on the quest by very different motives. The Puritans in New England, the Friends in Pennsylvania, the Catholics in Maryland, the Huguenots in New York and South Carolina, were exiles for conscience' sake, or were eager to practice their faith under freer conditions. The Dutch came to New York to further their fortunes, as did many men in all the colonies.

AMERICAN IDEALS

There were also ne'er-do-weels who had exhausted the patience of their friends at home and were sent to America with the hearty good wishes of those who were glad to be rid of them; and there were, as in all colonies, many restless and reckless spirits who hoped to find in the New World the freedom from restraint which the Old World imposed on them.

III

POSSESSING THE CONTINENT

THE thirteen English-speaking colonies in North America were, like Australia and New Zealand to-day, experiment stations in the science of government. They were ruled from a country three thousand miles distant in space and two months in time; and, long after they had become independent, communication with England was tedious, uncertain and perilous. The people of the leading colonies, New England and Virginia, brought to the New World strong convictions with regard to freedom of opinion and conduct; their presence in the wilderness was a protest against existing conditions in England. They had no common theory of the way in which they should be ruled, but they had escaped from some form of oppression or of repression; the foundations of their faith in the old order of things had been rudely shaken. They were shut off from those influences of daily association which are more powerful than law or force in keeping men together in political or social organization. They were fighting for existence with the consciousness, which deepened as time went on, that the home countries gave them little thought, and that their fortunes were in their own hands.

The colonists had also a keen sense of their own importance; they were aggressive in temper, or they would not have been pioneers; they were building new communities under conditions which compelled them to act independently, not only of the home government, but — for a time at least — of one another. They needed very skillful and sympathetic direction from London and, as a rule, they were under the management of men who had neither knowledge of the conditions nor that imagination which is one of the highest qualities of statesmanship.

For this blindness the age was largely responsible. The accepted idea of a colony was that it existed to enrich the home country;

POSSESSING THE CONTINENT

that as little as possible was to be given to it and as much as possible taken out of it. The needs and feelings of the colonists were of no importance to the distant government. The policy of exploiting colonies for the benefit of the home country was axiomatic. In this way Spain dealt with all her colonies in the New World, taking from them vast revenues and governing them by royal favorites, soldiers of fortune, ruined noblemen and speculators. In this way France ruled her colonies in the north, treating the vast tracts of country out of which her brave explorers and priests had created a new France as a pawn in the game of international diplomacy. The policy of managing colonies in their own interests now pursued by Japan in Korea, by the United States in the Philippines, and by England in Egypt had not so much as dawned on the minds of the men who governed the English colonies in America.

Nor had it occurred to them that colonial ministers and governors ought to be chosen for their ability and knowledge of conditions rather than for party services or as an expression of royal favor. The royal governors sent to Boston, New York, Jamestown, were, with some shining exceptions, men of stubborn will, dull imagination and a disposition to magnify their offices. Englishmen had thoroughly learned the importance of keeping the control of revenues and expenditures in their own control, and the colonial legislatures kept salaries, taxes and supplies in their own hands; a practice which set sharp limits to the powers of the royal governors, and kept both colonists and governors in a state of chronic irritation. The royal governors were dependent on the king, and the colonists were wise enough to keep a hold on them by control of the purse.

As time went on the colonies increased in population and in self-confidence, and their commercial interests began to conflict with those of the mother country. They were fast getting out of tutelage and resented a policy which treated them simply as sources of wealth for Great Britain. At the very time when wise statesmanship was sorely needed, the management of America's affairs

POSSESSING THE CONTINENT

fell into the hands of a group of politicians as dull and provincial in imagination as they were corrupt in political morals. George III was a man of honest heart, of limited intelligence and of a stubborn will. He held a high view of his prerogatives, regarded himself as the ruler of Great Britain, and, in working out his theory of personal government, was surrounded by pliant ministers who were his servants rather than his advisers. It ought to be remembered that the king and his ministers were dealing with conditions which were new in English history, that there were no precedents to guide them, that the policy pursued in America was in entire harmony with that pursued in England, and that, if foreign affairs had not forced themselves into the foreground, this policy would probably have led to popular resistance on the East as well as the West side of the Atlantic.

The root of the differences between the colonists and the government of George III was the arbitrary imposition of financial burdens on the colonists, and the arbitrary restriction of their trade and industries. The

AMERICAN IDEALS

colonists saw clearly that if the king secured control of their finances, their independence in the management of their internal affairs would be lost, and the fruits of the long struggle for liberty which had run parallel with English history would be sacrificed. It was not a struggle to save dollars and cents; it was a struggle to preserve hard-won rights. It was not then, nor did it become after war broke out, a struggle between the colonists and the English people; it was a fight between the colonists and the personal government of the king. There was widespread sympathy in England with the protests of the colonists; during the early years of the war, before France joined forces with the colonists, portraits of American generals hung in shop windows in English towns; and the most eloquent advocates of the rights of Englishmen beyond the sea were three or four great Englishmen in the House of Commons. The American Revolution was, in fact, a sequel to the English Revolution; an incident of tremendous and unexpected significance in the long fight for popular government in Eng-

POSSESSING THE CONTINENT

land; and the colonists would have been satisfied with a moiety of the freedom which has knit Canada and Australia to the British Empire.

The instinct of the king warned him that the contention of the colonists struck at the root of his un-English theory of government, and that if he conceded the soundness of the principle of "no taxation without representation," he would undermine the foundations of his power. He could carry on his policy of autocratic rule only by keeping a pliant majority in the House of Commons, and that majority depended on the command of elections in the "rotten boroughs" which a handful of voters represented in the Commons, while growing cities were entirely without voice in the government of the nation. If the American principle had been applied in England, the king would have lost his power and Chatham might again have been prime minister and the ruler of the empire.

The idea of separation from the mother country was in the minds of only a few far-seeing men when the struggle began, but it

AMERICAN IDEALS

was the logical and inevitable outcome of that struggle. To the great majority of leaders permanent separation was both unwelcome and impracticable; but as the war went on it became clear that the colonists must choose between subjugation and independence. Their condition in a struggle with a government of such resources as the British was desperate; but they were fighting on their own ground; they had able leaders and a man of great nature and great military skill at the head of their armies; they were opposed by a few generals of ability, but for the most part the British commanders were lacking in initiative, energy and flexibility. They underrated the fighting qualities of their opponents, and they obstinately refused to adapt their methods and tactics to the country in which they were an alien invading foe.

The war ended with the surrender of the British army at Yorktown in Virginia in 1781, though a treaty of peace was not signed until two years later. The colonists had won their independence, but they owed ten million

POSSESSING THE CONTINENT

dollars to creditors in France, Holland and Spain; their debts to their own people were heavy; business was prostrated; there was no central authority to levy and collect taxes; it was necessary to adopt new constitutions and organize new state governments. It was necessary, in a word, to reconstruct the local and state governments and to create some form of central government. During the eight years of war a Continental Congress, an emergency device, had supplied a central authority of a very ineffective and feeble kind. Articles of Confederation, also framed to meet an emergency, had defined the powers of this provisional body, which had performed some of the functions of government but was denied the exercise of essential governmental powers; taxes and import duties were left in the hands of the individual states; no bill passed by the Congress could become a law unless confirmed by a two-thirds vote of the states. The central government had no power to coerce a state which refused to contribute its share toward meeting the expenses of carrying on the government; and it had no

AMERICAN IDEALS

authority to represent the colonies in their relations with other governments. When the treaty with England was signed, the thirteen states were named as the contracting powers on the American side.

Those states were now independent, not only of Great Britain, of one another; they had stood together against a common foe, and when the danger which united them was past, they were held together loosely by their common needs, by their slowly acquired habit of acting together, and by their keen practical sense.

The genius of Washington, which had guided the colonists through appalling difficulties, led them another step in this journey towards independence. When the army was disbanded to become incorporated again into the citizenship of the country, as the great armies were received back into the vocations of peace at the end of the War between the States, he addressed a letter to the governors of the states pointing out the causes of the inefficiency of the general government during the war, and emphasizing the needs which

POSSESSING THE CONTINENT

must be met in organizing a permanent central authority. Such a government, he declared, must be based on an indissoluble union of the states; it must be empowered to lay and collect taxes and to provide for the payment of public debts; it must have authority to organize a system under which a citizen army should be at its command; a militia which could be called upon to preserve order and to defend the country against invaders. Such a central government, he said, could be secured only by laying aside local prejudices, sectional jealousies and mutual suspicion, and meeting the crisis in a spirit of concession and of willingness to make sacrifices for the sake of the general safety.

It was a crisis hardly less serious than that which had brought on the Revolution. The old colonies were thirteen small nations, largely ignorant of the temper and resources of one another; jealous of their rights; unaccustomed to any concerted action except that of defense. They were called upon to solve a problem which the Greek states with their immense intelligence did not succeed

AMERICAN IDEALS

in solving: to preserve local autonomy and independence and yet act as a nation under a central government. To the solution of this problem they brought the habit of free discussion of public affairs and of the management of local affairs, the political intelligence, and, above all, the political character, developed by centuries of Anglo-Saxon practice of political activity; and they had the wise and sober leadership of a group of statesmen who would have made any age memorable. The discussion was long and engrossed the attention of the people of the colonies from the close of the war in 1783 to the adoption of the Constitution in 1789. There were many conflicting claims for territory to be adjusted; and these were finally settled by an ordinance adopted in 1787; the first exercise of national sovereignty by Congress with the assent of the people of all the states, and under the provisions of which five great states in what is now the Central West were added to the original thirteen. This united action was an object lesson of immense importance to a group of states which were in danger of drifting into anarchy, if not of civil war.

In the Constitutional Convention which met later in the same year, there were fifty-five members, of whom thirty-two were men of college training, and many of these had been diligent students of the science of government. Four had conspicuously served the country and brought to the deliberations of the Convention wide experience, exact knowledge of existing conditions, and ardent devotion to the interests of the new nation: Washington, the foremost leader in war and a man of great and solid qualities of judgment; Benjamin Franklin, the personification, in his eighty-second year, of the practical sagacity and genius of the American; Madison, an expert in political knowledge, an admirable debater, of a capacious and luminous intelligence; and Hamilton, the most brilliant and fascinating figure of the Revolutionary period, who was later to develop an extraordinary and sorely needed genius for finance.

After four months of earnest and often

passionate discussion, the Convention presented a draft of a proposed constitution to the country, and the discussion was transferred from the Convention hall to the country at large and finally adopted by all the states in 1789.

Mr. James Bryce, whose "American Commonwealth" holds the first place among textbooks on the American political system, has said that "it ranks above every other written constitution for the intrinsic excellence of its scheme, its adaptation to the circumstances of the people, the simplicity, brevity and precision of its language, its judicious mixture of definiteness in principle with elasticity in detail." The wisdom of its framers was strikingly shown in making it a statement of principles and not a body of regulations. This feature has made it a vital and adaptable rule of political action instead of a mass of regulations which, in the nature of things, must always be largely temporary in their application. It has been the chief function of the Supreme Court which it created, to interpret its provisions and to apply them to changing conditions. The seventeen amendments which have been adopted since 1789 have supplemented rather than modified it.

This constitution offered a solution of the problem of combining local self-government with strong, effective central government, which may be regarded as the most important American contribution to the science of government. It created a powerful nation, and it preserved local autonomy; it combined the New England town meeting, the most elementary and radical form of democracy, with an effective national authority. The Greeks failed to take the step which might have preserved the practical independence of their brilliant cities without laying the country open to the foes who eventually destroyed her. The American colonies kept their autonomy and merged themselves in a nation by creating a permanent federation on a basis of local representation. They substituted for the earlier processes of absorption, or aggregation by conquest, unity of action through a representative government.

"Complete independence in local affairs,"

writes the author of "American Political Ideas," "when combined with adequate representation in the Federal council, has effected such a cohesion of interests throughout the nation as no central government, however cunningly devised, could ever have secured."

Under this system a government framed to conduct the affairs of four millions of people living along the Atlantic seaboard is managing the affairs of nearly one hundred million people and of a territory of continental magnitude. There is an undefined borderland, a "twilight zone," between the State and the nation, and there has always been and probably always will be, a broad difference of opinion respecting the division of powers between the States and the nation. The question of sovereignty was settled by a decisive war; the nation is supreme and the States constitute, not a group of independent sovereignties, but an indissoluble union in a nation. But the State lines remain intact; the affairs of each State are managed by that State without the interference of the Federal government. The wider action of the Federal government in recent years has been due to the enormous increase of interstate activities of all kinds, and has been necessitated by conditions with which the States are unable to deal.

The first election under the Constitution made Washington President of the United States, and the new government turned promptly to the many-sided and difficult work of organizing the machinery through which its policy could be carried out and its functions discharged. There were no precedents to guide the country, and there were wide differences of opinion to adjust; the various departments had to be created and set in operation; a financial policy had to be formulated with the utmost dispatch, for the finances of the country were in a chaotic condition; the Federal courts had to be constituted; and it was necessary to make a large number of appointments for important positions.

The danger point in the situation was the state of the finances; and fortunately the nation had in its service a man of financial genius. Hamilton was only thirty-two years of age, but he brought to his task technical knowledge of a high order; and, above all, though a man of extraordinary brilliancy, he had a firm will, solid judgment and a gift for mastering details. With astonishing rapidity, in a series of reports and bills, he laid before Congress and the country a scheme for the creation of a national bank, a mint and a currency; he funded the national and State debts, both foreign and domestic; and he provided sufficient income by laying taxes on the manufacture of spirits and duties on imports. He proposed a plan for the fostering of manufactures by a system of duties which may be regarded as the origin of the protection system in the United States. For Hamilton had the imagination of a statesman as well as the practical sagacity of a financier; he saw not only the need of putting the disordered finances of the nation on a sound basis, but of making provision for the development of its resources. Moreover, his plans had a political as well as a financial purpose; he aimed to create a group of men in all parts of the country who should be bound to the new government by their personal interests.

These radical and far-reaching measures at once brought out differences of opinion on fundamental constitutional questions, and these differences crystallized into the two theories which have divided Americans from the beginning of their history; and which, like the centripetal and centrifugal forces, have kept and will keep a balance between the relative powers of the nation and of the states.

The Federalists, under the leadership of Hamilton, held that the Constitution should be broadly interpreted and that the possession by the Federal government of such power as was necessary to make it effective and to secure the "general welfare" was implied. The Republicans, led by Jefferson, held to a strict construction of the Constitution and a sharp limitation of the powers and functions of the Federal government.

Other issues have risen from time to time, and other parties have appeared in the field, but this fundamental issue has always been involved. The parties have, however, changed names. The Federal party was succeeded by the Republican party, and that in turn may be succeeded by the Progressive party, which has declared for a still wider extension of the Federal power; the early Republicans have been succeeded by the Democrats, who have strenuously opposed such an extension of Federal authority. The tariff question, states' rights, secession or the right of a state to withdraw from the Union, the improvement of rivers and harbors, the building of canals, the reclamation and conservation systems, the regulation of industries by the national government, — these and many other questions of policy have all involved in one form or another the fundamental issue of the relative powers of the nation and the States.

Questions involving the interpretation of the Constitution were presented to the Supreme Court of the United States almost as soon as the government was organized, and under the leadership of chief justice John

POSSESSING THE CONTINENT

Marshall, — a man of commanding legal ability and force of mind, — the early decisions followed the lines of broad construction. With intervals of reaction the decisions of the court have consistently sustained the view of what have been called the "implied powers" of the Constitution, — the power to do whatever is necessary to make the Constitution effective, and to promote the welfare of the people who live under it.

The new nation began its career with a population of about four millions, living chiefly in thirteen states; it has now a population approximating one hundred millions, living in forty-eight states. It also exercises sovereignty over the Hawaiian Islands, the Philippines and Porto Rico. This growth has carried the center of population from the Atlantic seaboard to a point in the Central West.

The vast, and at that time unexplored, tract of country, west of the Mississippi River, had been claimed by early French explorers, who with incredible hardship and by an almost incredible physical endurance, had passed up the valley of the St. Lawrence, crossed to the Great Lakes, traversed the vast stretch of prairie to the Mississippi River, and made the first voyages down that river through the heart of the continent to the Gulf of Mexico. There is no more inspiring story of dauntless courage and heroic endurance than the record of French exploration in North America. This tract, of whose extent and resources all the countries interested in the settlement of the New World were ignorant, passed later under the control of Spain, and, still later, into the control of France. The Emperor Napoleon, engaged in a life-and-death struggle with England, and in great need of money, sold this territory to the United States in 1803 for fifteen million dollars; a purchase which doubled the area of the United States and put the nation in control of the waterway that made the sea accessible to the remote parts of half the continent.

This new territory was promptly explored, and the successful application of steam power to boats by Robert Fulton on the Hudson

POSSESSING THE CONTINENT

River made the Mississippi navigable at the psychological moment; as the invention of the cotton gin by Whitney, a New England schoolmaster, came into use at the hour when the South was ready for the enormous production of cotton which gave a decisive impulse to the industrial development of the country.

At the close of the war for independence, the first great wave of emigration poured through the passes of the Alleghany Mountains and spread over the valley of the Ohio, and of the chief eastern tributaries of the Mississippi, and laid the foundations on which a group of the most influential states in the Union — Ohio, Indiana, Michigan, Illinois, Iowa — were soon organized. The balance of political power passed, two generations later, into their hands. "The West," writes Mr. Bryce in the "American Commonwealth," "is the most American part of America." And the leading historian of the West has said that "the American spirit — the traits that have come to be recognized as the most characteristic — was developed in the new commonwealths that sprang into life beyond the seaboard. In these new western lands Americans achieved a boldness of conception of the country's destiny and democracy. The ideal of the West was its emphasis upon the worth and possibilities of the common man, its belief in the right of every man to rise to the full measure of his own nature under conditions of social mobility."

The population of the Central West and of the Mississippi Valley increased with such rapidity that in a single generation the population of one State in that section exceeded that of two of the oldest seaboard States. A vast tract of fertile country offered at nominal prices attracted enterprising, restless and dissatisfied people from the older sections, and the new country was settled by men who brought with them love of religion and of education, and habits of clean moral life, but who were ready for political and economic experiments and disposed to create an order of society in which there should be the largest liberty for individual activity.

As western Europe had, so to speak, pro-

POSSESSING THE CONTINENT

jected itself on America, so Eastern America projected itself on the West, and in each migration, the fundamental character remaining substantially unchanged, there was a distinct adaptation to new conditions and a distinct detachment from the older social standards. Virginia projected itself into Kentucky, and New England into the Central West. In 1817 a traveler on the national road, the first attempt of the Federal government to provide means of communication between the old and the new parts of the country, declared that Old America seemed to be breaking up and moving westward, and graphically described the procession of wagons, families and domestic animals flowing like a tide toward the Mississippi Valley. This great company of people became literally a floating population. Leaving the various roads by which they had come into the new country, they were carried to many destinations by large and small boats of many kinds, and by rafts of logs or lumber.

Arriving at his destination, the pioneer passed through the same stages through which

AMERICAN IDEALS

his ancestor from Europe had passed. He cut the trees and made a place for a home; he cut rings around the trees near his home, stopped the flow of the sap, gathered and burned the withered branches and planted his first crop among the stumps; his neighbors helping him when the house was to be raised or the logs rolled together to be burned. He purchased one hundred and sixty acres of land for two dollars an acre, paid fifty cents an acre in money, and had three or four years in which to pay the balance. The earlier settlers were often men without means, who, under a credit system which was both public and private, cleared and stocked the land, built homes, and earned by the hardest kind of work and saved by the most self-denying economy the money necessary to pay the debts they had incurred. There have probably never been such opportunities of creating wealth by hard work offered men without means as were open then, and for many years later, under the homestead laws, which made it the duty of the Federal government to sell public lands of enormous area on such

POSSESSING THE CONTINENT

easy terms as enabled the settlers to pay for their lands out of the income yielded by the lands.

The earliest settler was a backwoodsman, but he soon became or was followed by the pioneer farmer. The charred land became fertile, substantial houses took the place of log houses, sawmills were built, orchards planted, cattle multiplied, and little hamlets became villages, and villages grew into cities.

The same process, with the modifications introduced by slavery, was repeated in what is sometimes called the Southern South, — the territory which borders on the Gulf of Mexico. The lower valley of the Mississippi was settled, not only by poor folk allured by the chances of fortune under easy conditions, but by prosperous planters, with trains of slaves, packs of hunting dogs, and the habits and comforts of plantation life.

In 1830 there was a vast unoccupied country west of the Mississippi River. The prairies were a sea of flowers to the great plains whose aridity created what was called on the old maps The Great American Desert, now

AMERICAN IDEALS

smiling with fertility as the result of irrigation. The plains ended at the foothills of the Rocky Mountains, and constituted a territory which now supplies wheat, corn and cattle for the consumption of a considerable part of the world. A large part of this territory was claimed by Spain, including what are now the states of Texas, California, Arizona, Colorado, Utah and Nevada. Fur traders had long found their way through the defiles of the mountains to the Pacific coast; and trade with the Indians, started by the French, had been carried on in Indian villages and at trading posts on the Great Lakes and the upper Mississippi. Exploration went steadily forward, and half a dozen trails pierced the wilderness. Far-seeing men began to understand the enormous value of this territory to the nation, which had reached the Mississippi River. The Floridas had been purchased from Spain, and Louisiana from France; serious boundary disputes with Great Britain had been settled and had brought the Far Northwest under American control. Texas won its independence from Mexico and later

POSSESSING THE CONTINENT

was admitted as a state; a war with Mexico ended in a forced sale to the United States of a territory now divided into six states. Many Americans feel that this war, brought on as part of the policy of extending slavery, is the one war waged by the United States which was neither necessary nor just; but a glance at the map will show that the territory for which the United States paid eighteen million dollars was an integral part of the national domain, and must have come sooner or later under the American flag.

In 1848, the year in which peace was made with Mexico, gold was discovered in California, and at the end of twelve months there were a hundred thousand gold seekers on the ground; hardy, adventurous or reckless men, who had come overland by the trails, across the Isthmus of Panama, or in sailing vessels around Cape Horn.

At the close of the War between the States, the second great movement westward carried an active, eager population across the plains in long trains of prairie wagons, upon which from time to time the more warlike Indians made fierce attacks; and during this period there were many serious outbreaks which required the free use of considerable bodies of troops for the protection of immigrants. The latest chapter in the story of the futile attempt to keep the aggressive races out of a continent which had been the hunting ground of a few hundred thousand Indians was written in massacre and expulsion in the three decades which followed the close of the war; a struggle now happily ended by a just and generous policy toward the tribes, which still number in all probably two hundred thousand.

Meantime frontier towns were becoming thriving cities, mining camps permanent settlements, and vast farms were raising wheat on an unprecedented scale in the Northwest. The first of the transcontinental railroads sent the prairie wagon to the museum and the frontier to the Pacific coast. The task of settling the continent, begun at Jamestown on the Atlantic coast in 1607, was completed three centuries later on the Pacific coast; the development of the resources of the continent has as yet found no limit.

IV

PROVINCIAL AMERICA IN LITERATURE

UNLIKE other literatures, American literature had no childhood; no morning stories, so to speak; no local myths, traditions, marvelous tales of the beginnings of things; no songs of valor and adventure like the "Nibelungenlied," the "Chanson de Roland," the tale of Beowulf, the cycle of Arthurian legends. America is a new country, but the Americans are an old people; they began the experiment of living together not quite three centuries ago, in a historical age, which had not laid all the old ghosts to rest nor discarded all the ancient superstitions, but which wrote diaries and statistical reports rather than tales of love and chivalry, and listened to sermons, theological discussions and parliamentary debates, rather than to fairy stories and legends of heroes and gods. Such stories in some form it would doubtless have created in spite of its heavy daily tasks, since the imagination never entirely resigns its activity to the reason or to the hands; but it already possessed them in two or three literatures. When the American colonists began to write poetry and essays they showed early familiarity with the brood of celestial beings who had flitted from one early literature to another and found shelter wherever men loved beauty or conceived of truth as a living thing and not an abstract proposition. They were acquainted with the gods and goddesses whose names starred English or French poetry; and, later, when the most pressing work of settlement had been done and there was more leisure, they made classical allusions with the ease of the old-time university-bred men.

In the days when the little communities in the New World were in the most complete isolation, the children still heard the ballads which had formed a popular literature in English homes for many generations. "Chevy Chase," the most stirring of them all,

PROVINCIAL LITERATURE

which the chivalrous Sidney said moved him like a bugle call, was familiar to them. These old songs of the people were preserved and passed on, as the tide of settlement advanced, by word of mouth, and suffered many changes in the process of migration. In the great mountain region which extends from North Carolina westward to Tennessee and Kentucky, and includes parts of seven states, a population of nearly two million people have been isolated, until within the present generation, from the country about them, by lack of physical means of communication. Among these mountain people the old ballads brought over from England in the seventeenth and eighteenth centuries are recited with slight local adaptations, and words in use in England in Chaucer's time, and long since obsolete, are in common use. But in the face of great perils, and under the strain of great hardships, winged songs and tales of fantasy seemed like the toys of childhood.

In New England the earliest Americans were absorbed in an attempt to establish what they believed to be the kingdom of righteousness in the world, and to save their souls by shaping human law in conformity with divine law; in New York they were content with the beauty and fertility of the new country to which they had come from Holland, and with moderate prosperity and a pleasant social life; in Virginia vast tracts of fertile country, with access to fine rivers, made the rapid cultivation of great estates possible, and speedily developed a country life with many accessories of hospitality, sport and training in the management of large properties and the handling of large numbers of men.

Many of the early settlers both North and South were men of education; they brought with them memories of the colleges at Oxford and Cambridge, and the habits of reading men. There were collections of books in the homes of the colonists. William Brewster, one of the foremost men in the Plymouth Colony, was a man of gentle birth and breeding; he was born in a great manor house; he had been a student at Cambridge; he had held important positions at the Court of

PROVINCIAL LITERATURE

Queen Elizabeth, and he left a collection of several hundred volumes; a prominent member of the colony of Connecticut had a library of a thousand volumes, practically every volume of which must have been brought from Europe; John Harvard made a bequest of three hundred books to the University which bears his name. But there was very little literature in the sense of belles-lettres in these New England collections; they were largely made up of theological treatises and books on personal religion.

In Virginia there was a larger representation of the Greek and Latin classics and, later, of the standard English writers of the eighteenth century; but serious books, devoid of literary quality but dealing at great length and in the most dogmatic spirit with the religious interests and experiences of the times, greatly predominated. Calvin's "Institutes" might stand neighbor to Ovid's "Metamorphoses" on the shelves, but was more likely to find itself between the "Practice of Piety" and "Christ's Combat with Satan." In a few houses Bacon's "Advancement of Learn-

AMERICAN IDEALS

ing," Montaigne's "Essays" and Brown's "Religio Medici" were within reach. A copy of *Macbeth* was catalogued in Virginia in 1699, but no copy of Shakespeare's Plays is known to have existed in New England during the seventeenth century, nor was any reference made to him by an American writer during that century.

The English language, which is now the vernacular of two nations of world-wide activities and is heard in all countries, was the speech of a people isolated, in large measure, from intimate European contact and influence; it had been used by the foremost modern poet, who died nine years after the first English settlement in America; but dialects were still spoken in its home, it was regarded by scholars as lacking dignity and precision, and Latin was still the language of scholarship. This language went to America with the earliest settlers; many of whom were, as in all migrations, people of great energy but of slight education. The splendid flowering of the literary genius of the English people in the seventeenth century might have

PROVINCIAL LITERATURE

taken place in Japan, so far as the American colonists were concerned. Many of the most intelligent among them would have regarded the plays of Shakespeare and his contemporaries and the excursions of Edmund Spenser into fairyland as either frivolous or corrupting; others were too sternly fighting against hunger and the Indians to find either interest or profit in imaginative writing. The voyage across the Atlantic was long and perilous; ships were few; and the ocean was a barrier between the old and the new worlds which made the isolation of the colonies almost complete.

The colonists clung desperately to their language and made little attempt to adapt it to new conditions. They called a half-naked Indian ruler of a little company of painted savages, in a little village of wigwams which could be moved in a night, a king or an emperor, and an untutored Indian girl, in the scantiest garb and without possessions of any kind, a princess. They gave the birds which sang around their little communities the names of the birds that sang in Eng-

AMERICAN IDEALS

lish lanes and meadows; and for several generations American poetry was full of allusions to nightingales; and the "robin redbreast," the familiar companion of the humblest English homes, gave his name to an American thrush of entirely different shape and coloring. Later, when they acquired the sense of ownership, they became more inventive. They borrowed from the Indians such words as "sachem," "wigwam," "potato"; and they gave the birds descriptive names — the bluebird, the mocking bird, the catbird, the humming bird. In the widely separated colonies, as in the provinces in older countries, marked differences of idiom and pronunciation developed and have persisted in modified form to this day; so that it is not difficult for a trained ear to detect the accent of localities in the speech of strangers. As a matter of fact, many of those phrases which are broadly described as Americanisms are survivals of old English idioms fallen into disuse in the mother country, but remembered by her children beyond seas. Popular phrases, and especially those

PROVINCIAL LITERATURE

compact deposits of experience and observations which we call proverbs, in which Japan is so rich, were carried across the Atlantic by the earliest settlers and started on a new career on that advancing frontier of civilization which was to move westward for almost three centuries and to produce picturesque phrases and picturesque characters in prodigal profusion.

The intellectual situation in the colonies for a full century after the settlements at Jamestown in 1607 and in Plymouth Bay in 1620 may be briefly stated: communities of men and women from England, France and Holland whose exceptional independence, energy and self-reliance gave them certain formative characteristics in common were scattered along the Atlantic seaboard over a territory fifteen hundred miles long; these communities were fed from time to time by other colonists of a kindred temper; they were making homes for themselves in a country of whose climate and resources they were ignorant; they were surrounded by alert, cunning and revengeful foes; they were compelled to build their government and civilization from the foundations. A vast majority of these colonists spoke the English of the seventeenth century, and a small minority acquired it by force of circumstances; a small number of men of education and of women of high breeding were in every colony, but the population was made up largely of people of small means and meager opportunities. They were isolated from the intellectual movements and interests of the Old World, and engrossed in practical work which could be neither evaded nor postponed.

These people, full of the energy, independence and daring which had separated them from their fellows in the Old World and inspired them to take "the hazards of new fortune" in the wilderness, were not without records of their faith, of their history, of their race experiences. They came from races which had already used in a great way that form of expression which we call literature. Separated, as they were, from Europe in one of its most brilliant periods of literary expression, they brought with them a heritage

PROVINCIAL LITERATURE

of great memories, of heroic histories, of those creations of the imagination which reveal the genius of a race; they were inspired by religious or political convictions deep and vital enough to send them in voluntary exile; or they were driven by the love of adventure to brave all manner of perils on an unexplored continent. They were not, therefore, a company of materialists bent on trade or plunder, who found in trade or conquest an adequate expression of this spirit. For the most part they were men and women of exceptional energy, and the spiritual qualities they brought with them had already found expression in literature as well as in action.

Moreover, they had one classic of the greatest vitalizing power with them. The sixty-six books of history, prophecy, lyric poetry, symbolic fiction, narrative and biography which are bound together in the English Bible had been translated with wonderful skill at the very moment when the English language was a fountain of fresh and vital speech, and had passed into the hands of the English people. Published four years after the founding of Jamestown, this body of literature which English-speaking peoples call "The Book," passed into the hands of people to whom no other book had reached, became so embodied in the English language that it seems an integral part of that language, and was so thoroughly absorbed by the people as a whole that it has largely shaped ethical, political and social organizations and life wherever the English language is spoken.

The air of the age stimulated both the imagination and the passion for action; men were full of eager curiosity about the Far East and the Far West; but the West was so new and so strange they saw in it the old dreams of youth and wealth come true. They had been so intent on discovering new highways to the East that for many years their chief interest was not in exploring the new land in the Far West, but in finding the water courses through it which would furnish channels for their ships; and when, after many expeditions, they were forced to recognize the fact that they had uncovered, not an island, but a continent, they regarded it chiefly

PROVINCIAL LITERATURE

as an obstacle to free intercourse with the East. To the dream of finding a westward passage to Japan and China succeeded the dream of discovering mines of inexhaustible wealth and fountains of youth in America. The sailors who went with the explorers brought back tales which, after the manner of sailors' tales, suffered a "sea-change into something rich and strange." The native women in the new countries were described as "wearing great plates of gold covering their whole bodies like armor," pearls were to be found in heaps in native houses, and in these houses there were columns of gold and silver. Every returning voyager was expected to report something new and wonderful, and this expectation was rarely disappointed. In the sixteenth century the imagination was as daring as the spirit of discovery.

The contrast between the America of imagination and the America of fact was tragic in its completeness. The earliest colonists were compelled to fight desperately to maintain a foothold in the country. They were decimated by diseases which they did not

AMERICAN IDEALS

know how to avoid or to treat; they suffered from hunger, cold and heat; they were watched by relentless enemies; they were neglected by those at home who ought to have succored them in distress and given them the moral support of sympathy. This failure was due, not to lack of right feeling, but to the disparity between great schemes and rudimentary organization. The colonists were practically thrown on their own resources; a discipline which developed not only their capacity for taking care of themselves, but their independence of the mother country.

When people are building homes to shelter themselves from the elements, digging and planting to keep themselves from starvation, and cutting loopholes in their log houses and carrying guns to their work to protect themselves from sudden attacks by Indians, they have little need of expression and less opportunity to develop it. Their vitality went into their work and their imagination into their religion and into the further discovery of the world around them. The communities

PROVINCIAL LITERATURE

were separated by long stretches of unoccupied country, communication was slow and dangerous, and there was no common consciousness to express. Under such conditions the arts must wait on life, and in the New World life had many things to do before it could make time and room for art.

The earliest books written in the colonies were, therefore, theological discussions, narratives of religious experience and reports of the country. They were written for a purpose and were as free from the art of writing as the rude houses of the country folk were from the spirit of architecture. The first book written in that part of America which is now the United States was an account of adventures in Virginia by Captain John Smith, — a man of great courage and ability and of a bold and highly inventive imagination, whose habit of boasting has discredited his really great services to the colonists at Jamestown. As the redoubtable Captain grew older in years, his adventures grew more wonderful in the telling, but his report of conditions in Virginia has historical value.

AMERICAN IDEALS

At the end of a century and a half, common grievances against the mother country and common perils at home began to develop a consciousness of common interests in the different colonies. The intervening territory had been filling up with settlers, means of communication had become regular, there was much more regular intercourse, suggestions of coöperation between the colonies for defense were in the air, so to speak, and a plan for joint action, brought forward by Benjamin Franklin on the eve of what is known as the French and Indian War, was widely discussed.

In that war, which established English rule in Canada, all North America was brought under English authority and the original colonists largely relieved of danger from Indians; several of the colonies coöperating in furnishing men and money. Fifteen years later they were to stand together in the attempt to establish their independence of the British government. In the meantime they had begun to develop that consciousness of common need and experience

PROVINCIAL LITERATURE

which makes the subsoil of literature, and the first expression of this consciousness took the form of argument, discussion, satire. The War of the Revolution was preceded by a war of words. The grievances of the colonists, which had been many times laid before the authorities in England, found more emphatic and comprehensive statement. The colonists began to define their position for their own guidance and to make their appeal to the enlightened opinion of Europe. They examined the grounds of their protests more critically, strove to formulate the principles on which they rested their claims, and searched English history for precedents for their course. The discussion took a wide range and involved ultimately the fundamental political principles which the English people had slowly worked out in their struggle for participation in government. Men of ability came to the front in several colonies. Samuel Adams, a man of great energy of character and style in the Massachusetts colony, wrote a stirring and strongly phrased defense of the rights of the colonists against

AMERICAN IDEALS

arbitrary government by the group of irresponsible ministers who surrounded an honest but narrow-minded and obstinate king. As time went on, the feeling became passionate; there was no thought of independence as yet, save among a few radical leaders, but there was a growing sense of injustice and a growing determination to secure for Englishmen beyond the sea the rights enjoyed by Englishmen at home.

Americans and Englishmen, looking back on that great debate and on the long struggle in which it ended, now see clearly that the American Revolution was part of the struggle for popular rights in England; and not until other elements entered the field, notably the assistance of France, did the war become popular with the English people. For many years it was a conflict between the colonists and the group of incompetent or corrupt politicians who formed what was called the King's Party, and that conflict was waged as bitterly in the British Parliament as in English possessions in America. There was a flood of pamphlets in the colonies, and there

PROVINCIAL LITERATURE

were great speeches in Parliament, where the case of the colonists was stated with noble eloquence by a group of the greatest statesmen in English history, notably by Lord Chatham and Charles James Fox; men of the highest oratorical ability and of a lofty patriotism, whose fight for popular rights involved a courage and resolute persistence hardly paralleled by that of the colonists themselves.

This discussion on both sides of the Atlantic rose to the dignity of literature; and the work of John Adams, of James Otis, of Thomas Jefferson — of whom James Russell Lowell, the distinguished poet and critic, said that he doubted if America had produced a better thinker or writer—and of many other men, came to the front in this discussion, which not only produced the first writing of literary quality in America, but developed a sense of common danger and common conviction among the colonists and prepared the minds of men for united action when the crisis came. Deep feeling and passionate conviction gave these pamphlets and addresses and the speeches of men like Patrick Henry, the Virginian who struck off in the heat of oratory some phrases that became watchwords in the struggle, — "if this be treason, make the most of it," "as for me, give me liberty or give me death," — an eloquence which invested them with those qualities of beauty of phrase or of authority of thought which we associate with literature. Both discussions and speeches had immediate ends in view, but these ends were served by an appeal to principles so fundamental in the development of society that what was fashioned for the need of the moment took on the dignity and significance of things that endure for all time.

At the end of the war the colonists found themselves facing perils almost as great as those through which they had passed. They had secured independence, but they were without a government. It was then that the long discipline and training of a people who had been in the habit of governing themselves in local affairs showed their organizing power; during the critical years between 1783

PROVINCIAL LITERATURE

and 1789 the colonies went on with their work and life by virtue of the political character and habits of the people. The central authority, created by the temporary expedient of Articles of Confederation, was so devoid of power either of initiative or of regulation, that it maintained but a shadow of authority. There was no basis for general credit, no common currency, no uniformity of law; the colonies had still a very imperfect knowledge of one another, their differences of religious faith and practice and of social custom were many, there were bitter local jealousies and serious disputes with regard to boundaries. More immediately important and perilous were the wide and deep differences of opinion as to what kind of government should be created: a government of restricted powers, which should deal with the general interests of the colonies under limitations so many and so great as to make it little more than an advisory body; or a government invested with power to make laws binding on all citizens and to enforce them. The fundamental question, the full scope of which only a few men saw at the time, was: shall there be confederation of sovereign states or a nation? That question was not to be settled until after another long debate and another and more destructive war.

The country became a vast debating society, and the Constitution which was finally framed was fashioned in the fire of that long and earnest discussion. The spectacle of a widely settled population, organized under fully developed local governments and of mature and strongly held political convictions, discussing the nature and scope of the government under which they should live, was new in the history of the world and was the mental preparation for the making of a nation. In that discussion many of the ablest men in the country came to the front. Some of them, like Hamilton, had made reputations in military service; others, like Jefferson, showed themselves masters of the history and principles of government. Among those who advocated a strong central government, none was more influential than Alexander Hamilton, the most brilliant and engaging

PROVINCIAL LITERATURE

personality of the period, the intimate friend of Washington; a man who showed, later, genius of a high order as a financier. His contributions to this momentous debate, with those of Madison, who became the third President of the United States, appeared in the newspapers of the day and probably exerted more influence on public opinion than any other statements of the case; and *The Federalist*, the title of the volume in which they were subsequently issued, is one of the foremost American political classics. The leading spirit of the party which urged a government of rigidly restricted powers was Thomas Jefferson, who succeeded Washington in the Presidency; a man of broad general education, of cultivated tastes and of radically Democratic principles; a student of French history and literature, sympathetic with the popular movement in that country. Jefferson was a man of vision rather than a practical statesman; he was the founder of the University of Virginia, one of the foremost institutions of the highest class in the country. He had great charm of manner, both in person and in speech; and the name of no one of the founders of the government is more frequently heard than his in the political discussions of to-day.

These two long discussions disseminated political ideas in all the colonies and formed in Americans that habit of political debate which very largely gives popular government its educational quality; and, while neither pamphlets nor speeches belong to belles-lettres, they expressed for the first time what was to become the national consciousness and are the earliest American writings of permanent interest as literature.

The United States created by the adoption of the Constitution in 1879 began its career with a population of about four million people, scattered through thirteen colonies. A nation had been called into existence, but in name only. There was a small group of men who distinctly foresaw the future development of the national idea and of the natural resources, but the vast majority of the subjects of the new government were still in what may be called the colonial condition of mind; they

PROVINCIAL LITERATURE

had severed political connections with the Old World, but they were still dependent on that world for literature, for art, for music, for social tradition, for fashions of dress. Their tastes and interests were provincial and were to remain provincial for a generation. Save in the form of orations, political discussion and state papers, they were without a literature. They had, however, produced two writers who were, to quote Matthew Arnold's happy phrase about Emerson, — "friends of the spirit." Jonathan Edwards, a preacher of terrifying power who turned the white flame of divine purity into a consuming fire for the evil, was a man as unlike some of the doctrines he preached as the practices of some people who call themselves Christians is unlike the religion they profess. He was at heart a mystic, and, like all mystics, he lived in devout communion with spiritual thoughts and beings. In an age in which the sense of sin was abnormally developed, the sensitive imagination of this teacher of the immutable will of God as the supreme truth known to men pictured with startling vividness the fate of those who refused to accept that will. His mind was, however, eminently philosophical and his "Freedom of the Will," written twenty years before the Revolution, has been called "the one large contribution which America has made to the deeper philosophic thought of the world." In grasp of thought and power of logic that statement still remains true, although America has since produced thinkers of greater subtlety and originality.

Edwards was a man of the New England type; ardently religious and as ardently convinced that the truth of religion could be finally and dogmatically stated in philosophic terms. John Woolman, on the other hand, was a man of the Middle Colonies, of humble origin and of slight education. He was a member of the Community of Friends, who had come into existence in England as a protest against what they called worldliness, who held that the human spirit is in communion with the divine spirit without the instrumentality of priests or temples or church organization. They listened for the Inner Voice which

PROVINCIAL LITERATURE

speaks in every man's soul; they were mystics in religion and individualists in society. They dressed soberly, and were notable for honesty in their dealings, though by no means lacking in shrewdness; they were simple in manner and speech; and they held war in abhorrence. It was among them that the first organized opposition to the institution of slavery, then generally established in the colonies, had its rise.

Of this company of unworldly people devoted to the life of the spirit, John Woolman was a notable type. He was also an example of what the human spirit, purified and refined by unselfish love of men, can accomplish. He was an illiterate tailor, but he wrote in a style of rare purity and grace; he hated slavery, but he loved the slave owner. He was studious by nature and gave his leisure hours to books; and he was much given to long walks and to meditation. "I found it safest," he said, "for me to live in private and keep these things sealed up in my own breast." His "Journal," begun in his early maturity and continued until his death in 1772, is a record of his inner life, of his thoughts on slavery, and of his prophetic views of the labor question. It is in no sense a great piece of literature, but it has the quality of literature and has found very appreciative recognition among lovers of good writing in England. Franklin's "Autobiography," although written in part before the Revolution, was not published until the year following the adoption of the Constitution.

During the three or four decades that followed the winning of independence, two marked tendencies developed: a pronounced antagonism to everything English, and a pronounced admiration for everything American. Patriotism was as much a matter of hating as of loving. The hardships, perils and victories of the Revolution were still fresh in the minds of the people, and the men who had endured and triumphed were still among them. Intercourse with the Old World was still slow, hazardous and expensive; the legacy of antagonism to England bequeathed by the Revolution had been augmented by unfortunate incidents of the second war with that

PROVINCIAL LITERATURE

country which began in 1812; there was a widespread habit of glorifying the men who had part in the first struggle. A popular mythology of heroic proportions sprang up, and men who had never been conspicuous to their comrades in the field took on heroic proportion in the piping times of peace, especially if they happened to be candidates for public office. America was still provincial, although it was on the eve of becoming sectional. It was still isolated from the Old World, although it was on the eve of reknitting the broken ties of friendly intercourse and coming again into relations with it.

It is an interesting and significant fact that this reëstablishment of severed relations came largely through a group of men of letters and of scholars. There had been vigorous writing in America, but it had been so far the literature of information, of theology, of politics. The literature of imagination, of humor, of sentiment, began in New York, the chief city of the most cosmopolitan of the old colonies now become States, and the future metropolis of the nation. It was then a pleasant city of about twenty-five thousand inhabitants. It lay between two rivers, and it had a spacious and beautiful harbor. One of these rivers, the Hudson, had not only great scenic, but, for its time, great historic, interest. The men and women who originally settled it came from Holland; they were followed in due time by a large migration from England; and, still later, French Huguenots, expelled from their own country on account of their faith, came in large numbers and settled in New York and the country which lies east of it on Long Island Sound. Other races were represented in smaller groups, and when the colonies became a nation, eighteen or twenty languages were spoken in New York. Its citizenship was less distinct in type than that of New England or of the Southern Colonies. It was less serious in temper than the colonies to the east of it and more cosmopolitan than those to the south, which were largely agricultural in occupation. It was a commercial city, and, although it had suffered greatly during the war, it was not so sharply separated in feeling from the mother country.

PROVINCIAL LITERATURE

In this city which has always held its gates wide open to the world, Washington Irving was born in the year in which the British troops reëmbarked for England. He declined to go to college, read law and literature, and made his first visit to Europe in 1804. He was a born loiterer and observer, and he was the first American after the separation to see England with the old-time affection and under the spell of the old-time associations. Two years later he returned to his native city to join a group of high-spirited and vivacious young men of satirical temper in the writing of a series of witty comments on men and manners in the metropolis after the manner which Addison and Steele had made familiar in the *Spectator*. These papers revealed Irving's humor, his sentiment and his felicity of style. They were followed by the publication of a book of unique quality in American writing, a "History of New York," broadly burlesquing the incidents of its early history, and the characters of its early men. The narrative had the manner of serious history, but it was a piece of good-natured but audacious fun-making. Published in 1809, it made a great sensation locally, but its readers did not know that it marked the beginning of American literature. It was the first book of quality and feeling written by an American. It reminded Walter Scott of Dean Swift, but Irving belonged to the school of Addison and Goldsmith.

In 1815 he went to Europe a second time and did not return to New York until 1832; in the meantime he had written several volumes of essays and sketches, — a "Life of Columbus," charming studies of the Alhambra, and the "Conquest of Granada." None of his books was of the first rank, but all had the quality of literature, and the dates of their appearance and their influence on American Letters give them permanent importance. In two volumes of delightful sketches, "Bracebridge Hall" and the "Sketch Book," Americans came again under the spell of things and places dear to their ancestors. Westminster Abbey rose before them again in all the majesty of its ancient architecture and of its august memories; they heard again the peal-

PROVINCIAL LITERATURE

ing of bells from the venerable churches in which their ancestors had worshiped; they saw the home of Shakespeare; they enjoyed again the comforts of old inns and shared the hospitality of old homes.

Under the spell of Irving's charming power of description, an England that had largely faded from the memory of men and women in the New World became once more the mother country of their language, their religion, of their political ideals and social habits.

Irving did more than this: in the "Legend of Sleepy Hollow" and in "Rip Van Winkle" he gave to Americans two characteristic legends; he prepared the way for American fiction; and he furnished a convincing answer to Sidney Smith's question, "Who reads an American book?" For these books found many lovers in the Old World, and years afterwards Thackeray called Irving "The First Ambassador Whom the New World of Letters sent to the Old."

This reknitting of the old ties was also one of the services rendered by Longfellow, a man of the best New England stock and education, to whom the opportunity of travel and study in Europe came early; who became an accomplished linguist and returned to teach the modern languages in Harvard University and to become the most popular of American poets. He was of a gentle and lovable nature, of a quiet charm of personality. He was a scholar ripened into a man of culture by wide acquaintance with art in various forms. Longfellow's sensitive imagination and historic sense made him one of the earliest of the many pilgrims who have gone back from the New World to the places and buildings associated with the earlier story of the races from which Americans are descended. His brother once said of him that the key to his character was sympathy. This quality, tempered by knowledge and reënforced by a pictorial imagination, made him an interpreter and a translator. He felt deeply the charm of ancient places, the fascination of old stories, the appeal of the self-denials, the romances and the heroisms of long ago; and in his verse Nuremberg, Prague, Salerno, Sicily, Switzerland, serve as backgrounds for happily retold

PROVINCIAL LITERATURE

legend, history or romance. Through the temperament of this poet of the affections Europe became again to many estranged Americans an ancestral home rich in the treasures of art and of memory.

Longfellow also drew freely on the traditions of his own country, and two of his most familiar narrative poems, "Evangeline," a story of the expulsion of the French from Acadia, in lower Canada, and their settlement in the extreme south, and "Hiawatha," an Indian legend of great beauty, have taken their places beside Irving's "Rip Van Winkle" and "Legend of Sleepy Hollow" as the most original legends that have their roots in American soil. He was the poet of the domestic affections and of childhood, and many of his short pieces are known by the school children of America. He was a gentle moralist, and, although lacking the highest gifts of inspiration, he put a brave and gentle philosophy of life into a few poems which have become an informal creed of faith and endeavor among all classes of people. His translation of Dante's "Divine Comedy" was

AMERICAN IDEALS

a labor of love as well as scholarly rendering of notable fidelity to the condensed and closely knit style of the greatest literary work of the Middle Ages. Longfellow's ease in giving happy expression to the common human experiences and aspiration has, since his death, somewhat obscured his real poetic gifts, and many critics have been content to give him place only among the popular poets; but this will not be his final position. His ballads and many of his sonnets reveal a poetic talent of a high order. Nor will it be forgotten that he was one of the little group of writers and scholars who put an end to the provincial isolation of America and made Americans conscious of the wealth of their racial heritage and of their place in the unbroken development of civilization.

In Longfellow's youth began that pilgrimage of aspiring young men from the American colleges to the German universities which contributed largely to the restoration of what may be called the intellectual equilibrium between the Old and the New World, and which greatly affected the educational aims

PROVINCIAL LITERATURE

and methods in the American colleges. The return of ardent young scholars like Bancroft, who wrote later the first authoritative history of the United States, and of Everett, the polished orator and publicist and president of Harvard College, marked the beginning also of the very definite influence of German thought and literature on American culture. With these young scholars and poets, Provincial America passed into Sectional America.

V
SECTIONAL LITERATURE

IN the year 1817, in the best-known American periodical of the time, there appeared a poem by a young man who had been born among the New England hills and was then studying law. "Thanatopsis" was the first notable poem from an American hand, and its author, William Cullen Bryant, was the first man to strike a new note in its poetry, which until that time had been slight, graceful and imitative, or satirical in mood. The population had doubled since the colonists gained their independence, and seven million people now called themselves Americans; they had settled the Atlantic seaboard, organized the country beyond the Alleghany Mountains into states or territories, acquired by purchase from France an immense section between the Mississippi River and the Rocky Mountains, maintained the national authority in the face of local insurrections and of threats

SECTIONAL LITERATURE

of secession north and south, fought a second time with Great Britain, built roads and canals, and laid the foundations of a great manufacturing prosperity.

The Provincial Period was at an end; the Sectional Period had begun. The country was in the condition of Italy in the early years of reunion, when men still called themselves Piedmontese, Venetians, Romans, Sicilians, rather than Italians. In the United States men and women thought of themselves first as New Englanders, Virginians, South Carolinians. The state consciousness was sharply developed and keenly sensitive in all matters of local interest or dignity; a national consciousness was yet to be born. The Northern States were rapidly developing manufacturing and demanded the protection of tariff legislation; the Southern States were largely given to agriculture and were opposed to any restrictions of trade. In the North one State after another had abolished slavery; in the South, where many men of great prominence foresaw inevitable trouble and the inevitable passing of the system, the economic needs of the new States on the Gulf of Mexico seemed to make slave labor a necessity. In the alignment of conviction on the fundamental question of the relative powers of the States and of the Federal government the people of the Southern States largely held to the sovereignty of the States, while a majority of the people of the North held that sovereignty resided in the nation.

These differences were in part reflected in differences of social ideal and habit, and in part reënforced by these differences. The rigid rule of religious discipline in New England had been greatly relaxed and the attempt to establish a government along the lines of the Jewish theocracy abandoned; but the Puritan emphasis on morals still held, and the widespread interest in religion was evidenced by the Unitarian protest against the Calvinistic conception of the nature of deity and of humanity. The people were, as a rule, of sober temper; industry and frugality were characteristic of the section; education was held in high regard, and was universal. The Middle Colonies were cosmopolitan in pop-

SECTIONAL LITERATURE

ulation, social life was freer, and there was little moral tension. English, French and Dutch, in New York, Swedes in New Jersey, Friends from England and Germans from the Rhine provinces in Pennsylvania, Englishmen of the Roman Catholic faith in Maryland, fostered tolerance of opinion and ease of mood. Englishmen of the aristocratic type, living like great English landlords, in Virginia; the descendants of the French Protestants in South Carolina; men of Spanish and French blood in Louisiana, — presented a broad contrast to the New England temperament and habit. Life on the plantation was, in its best estate, patriarchical in spirit; work was done by slaves; the landowners were hospitable and generous, given to sport and out-of-door life. When the question of restricting or extending slavery began to be seriously discussed about the time of the appearance of Irving and Bryant, there were distinct temperamental and political differences between the North and the South.

A great war was to be fought to the bitter end before a national literature could come into existence. Literature is primarily an expression, and, while prophetic notes are always heard in it, it cannot travel far ahead of the consciousness of the race that produces it. It is touched with visions of the future, but it is conditioned largely on the experience of the people who produce it. Provincial America produced little literature because, among other reasons, it had no experience to express and interpret. Sectional America produced a literature which was largely sectional in experience and feeling because there were as yet only pools of common consciousness, so to speak; the consciousness which has the breadth and reach of the sea, and its universality, could come only when the people of the States became the people of a nation.

This local consciousness first found expression in New York, where people had lived together long enough to have a store of common memories, of common habits, and of common ideals and hopes. Irving happily expressed the community feeling at the same time that he revived the sense of community with the Old World.

SECTIONAL LITERATURE

American landscape painters were impressed at the beginning by the vastness of the New World landscapes, and many of the early canvases were on a great scale. Bryant, though of classical education and familiar with English poetry, saw that he was in a new world. It is often said that magnitude has no significance for art; that quality alone counts. But we study a building not only with reference to its construction, but with reference to its situation; we do not put a small picture in a large frame, nor do we place a small building at the focal point of a great landscape. Now, in America, magnitude did count and will always count; to dismiss it as mere bigness — mass without organization — is a fatal blunder if one wishes to understand or to judge intelligently. For in America bigness is not inert; it is potential.

Bryant saw that Nature in the New World is not on the scale of a county or of a province, but of a continent. Matthew Arnold said that the American landscape was not interesting. It was a judgment possible only to a man who held that in landscape a certain

AMERICAN IDEALS

scale is absolute. But scale is relative; there is a scale for England and a scale for America; and each in its place is adequate and final. The American landscape does not lack beauty of detail; but it is molded on a great scale. If the continent could be seen in one all-embracing vision, it would show a massive structural plan; lines that sweep over a thousand miles; mountain ranges that run from the Arctic zone to the tropics; valleys cut by imperious rivers which, like the Colorado, flow a mile below the edges of what were its banks a million years ago; plains which, seen from the upper slopes of the hills, have the sweep of the sea, but with the wonder and mystery of sunlight modulated by vast distances; deserts stretching, shimmering in fierce light, from horizon to horizon. On a landscape of such range, with diversities of feature as striking as its extent, scale is the first and most obvious element; an element as susceptible of artistic treatment as the exquisite delicacy of miniature landscapes.

Bryant's imagination was not facile, his command of verse forms was limited, but the

SECTIONAL LITERATURE

majesty of an almost unsubdued continent gave him a sense of elemental things. Simplicity, vigor, love of untamed Nature, a primitive divination of the greatness of life in the companionship of Nature, give his work austere beauty. He knew Nature about his home as well, and his songs of flowers and birds are dear to Americans by reason of their beautiful rendering of things familiar to the eye, but full of mystery to the imagination. Like all the poets of his section, he could not escape the moral implications of life as the Puritan saw it, and the lines "To a Waterfowl," limned against the sky with something of the fidelity of a Japanese painter, became a parable of human destiny.

In Bryant three or four notes are sounded which have never been silent in American poetry: love of Nature, love of country, love of liberty, love of home. A large body of American poetry of the Sectional Period is dear to children, not because it was written for them, but because it deals with childhood, with life in the home, with the sorrows and joys of the school, the fields, the shaded streets, the brooks and the woods. This is preëminently true of the verse of Whittier, the Quaker poet, whose "Snow Bound" is the idyl of the old-time life on the New England farm, and whose songs of religion are tender and trustful psalms of faith in the divine love and care. In American schools on certain days one will hear "Skipper Ireson's Ride," or Longfellow's "Psalm of Life," or Lowell's "The First Snow," or Emerson's "Good-by, Proud World," or Dr. Holmes' "The Nautilus," or Bryant's "Death of the Flowers." Whittier was a farmer's son and knew the workers in the small New England towns. He was a poet of the people; his hatred of slavery made him preëminently a poet of freedom, and his poems during the long debate which preceded the war and during the four terrible years of conflict were notable for their undismayed faith in the victory of freedom.

The most accomplished New England writer and the most accomplished man of Letters whom America has so far produced, although a man of academic training and long academic association, was also a poet of democratic

SECTIONAL LITERATURE

instinct and sympathies; a lover of Nature, of the home and of freedom. In the later years of his life Lowell entered public life as the American Ambassador in London, where his delightful personality, his broad culture, his wit and a kind of new-world freedom, never obtruded but were never concealed, made him an ideal representative of his country. He had, too, a charming gift of public speech, and no one was heard with more pleasure on literary and commemorative occasions. A scholar in three or four literatures, Lowell had an intimate knowledge of the plain country folk of his section, the old-time Yankee, who, in foreign eyes, has become the typical American, although he was the product of a small section and represents the country as little as the mastodon represents the animal world of to-day. Lowell had many gifts, and his "Commemoration Ode" at the close of the war rose easily to a great national theme; but his most characteristic quality was humor, which he used with great effect in the years when the encroachment of slavery evoked increasing and determined resistance. The

AMERICAN IDEALS

"Biglow Papers" are in the Yankee dialect, and have all the Yankee shrewdness and the dry Yankee humor.

Emerson, the descendant of Puritan preachers and scholars, of a singular unworldliness of temper and a nature from which evil instincts seemed to be absent, an idealist, a reformer and a shrewd observer, who taught a philosophy of life which brought the simplest duties and tasks into harmony with the most daring aspirations, was a poet of a few notes of singular purity. He was chiefly a writer of essays, but half a dozen poems of his are likely to be remembered as long as any verse of his period. They are mystical, elusive, with not a little of Oriental thought in them; but they have a simplicity of form and a homeliness of imagery and illustration which make them as familiar as the stars and as splendidly remote from common things. To Emerson the highest thoughts were for domestic use, and he held nothing too sacred or too divine for human service. As a poet his range was limited, he lacked facility in the use of verse, and he lacked the fire and color

SECTIONAL LITERATURE

of temperament; but he had a few hours of inspiration, and in these hours he wrote half a dozen poems of spiritual insight and of original phrasing. A radical democrat in his conception of life as a spiritual opportunity open on equal terms to all men, Emerson regarded slavery as an almost incredible anachronism in the nineteenth century and on American soil, and assumed its extinction as inevitable.

Oliver Wendell Holmes was born in a colonial house within the grounds of the oldest American university. He was of the purest New England blood, and his mind was of the most distinctive New England type. He had thrown off, ancestrally, the rigid Puritan faith and practice, but he retained and expressed its moral health, its refinement of taste, its fastidiousness of personal association; he was an aristocrat of intellectual temper, with a genius for celebrating ancestral achievements and local customs. Goethe's *genius loci* stands beside the Ilm in the lovely park at Weimar; Dr. Holmes' *genius loci* may be found on Boston Common.

AMERICAN IDEALS

A teacher of medicine by vocation and not without distinction in that field, he was the creator of a new literary form in which fiction, narrative, philosophy and shrewd observation of life were dexterously fused into a vivacious, ingenious and suggestive narrative, half fact and half fable. His wit was quick, clean, neat; he lacked the broad, sympathetic quality of Lowell's humor. He was a poet of occasions, but his occasional verse has a vitality of feeling and of fancy which has survived the occasions. The lights were extinguished long ago, the diners have gone and the rooms are silent, but the celebrations of friendship, of loyalty to old affections, of tender memory of the dead, have become the commemorative songs of a later generation. Dr. Holmes' novels are original and entertaining, but they are the work of a versatile writer using fiction to express ideas and theories. Alone among the poets of his section, he lacked the temperament of the reformer, and the stormy times in which he lived affected neither his occupations nor his writing.

To New England and to the Sectional

SECTIONAL LITERATURE

Period belongs a prose writer of high distinction, whose place, in any critical estimate of the Puritan literature, is beside Emerson. The child of a long line of colonists, Hawthorne had great beauty of person, a reticence through which only a very few passed to intimate friendship, a brooding imagination and the habit of solitude. He was fortunate in his college associations, and ideally fortunate in his marriage with a woman of a sensibility as delicate as his own, but of great sanity of mind. In Miss Wilkins' stories of New England there are many lay hermits; men and women who live alone on the outskirts of villages or on remote farms, and have only the most casual relations with their fellows. These recluses are the victims of individualism become morbid; a type of temperament which closely approaches insanity. Hawthorne grew up in such a family, and might have taken refuge in solitude and silence but for an impulse to express himself which became imperative and the devotion of a wife who understood and helped him.

Later he lived in England and in Italy;

but, though his imagination was stimulated by Italian art and scenery, he was not greatly affected by either country. He was an observer of men and events, but was never on intimate terms with life. His intellectual detachment was as complete as his personal isolation in a period of great agitation. Those who were on terms of friendship with him found him singularly free from every kind of pretension, self-poised, acute in observation and power of analysis, and capable of complete absorption in his work. His wife speaks of him as simple, transparent, just, tender and magnanimous, and of a wonderful delicacy of nature. "Was there ever," she wrote, "such a union of power and gentleness, such softness and spirit, passion and reason?"

In all the New England writers, character bore so intimate a relation to genius and was so large an element in their work that it is impossible to deal with them simply as artists. They were first and always men of conviction, and art was to them a form of expression rather than a manner of life. But Hawthorne was primarily an artist. His earliest

SECTIONAL LITERATURE

experiments in writing were short sketches and shadowy stories; in which his imagination, not yet strong enough for constructive work, played with supernatural suggestions, morbid experiences, mysterious incidents. In many of these sketches there was obvious moralization, but it was in the interest of art rather than of ethical teaching. Hawthorne dealt habitually with the problems of conscience, not because he was a teacher of morals, but because these problems were part of his inheritance, and because they possessed him with a sense of their artistic potentiality. Many of these sketches were slight in substance and manner, but they had a kind of twilight beauty.

His longer stories are not novels; with the exception of the "Marble Faun" they are romances of the New England mind and temperament; and the "Marble Faun," wholly Italian in background and largely Italian in character, is pervaded by the spirit of the Puritans. The "Scarlet Letter," still the foremost story written by an American, deals with the problem of sin in its moral consequences with a penetration of analysis and a subtlety of perception that make it the classic study of the Puritan conscience. It is so full of shadows that we seem to be seeing tragedy on a half-lighted stage; but the sense of the grip of the offense on the offender is as unescapable as in Tolstoi's "Anna Karenina." The tale is steeped in a dusky splendor like the glow of cathedral windows at sunset; and the style has the reticence of suggestion and the compass of complete expression. In "The House of Seven Gables," the "Blithedale Romance" and the posthumous tales, later aspects of New England temperament and individualistic attitude of mind are studied and sketched with a vitality of imagination which makes it impossible to separate Hawthorne's style from his subject matter.

To the period of Sectional America belong two or three writers widely known outside their own country. Cooper divides with Irving the honor of giving American writing its larger initial impulse, and of making Europe aware that the young communities beyond the sea had something significant to

SECTIONAL LITERATURE

express and knew how to express it. American poetry dates from the publication of Bryant's "Thanatopsis" in 1817 and American fiction from the appearance of "The Spy" in 1821. Stories had been published in America, but they were experiments rather than achievements; and while some of them, the tales of Charles Brockden Brown especially, have historical interest, they do not count in a general survey of American literature. Cooper does count; he is still read in all parts of the world, and for many decades in all parts of Europe boys have organized themselves into bands of Cooper Indians.

The future novelist spent his childhood on the shores of a lake of great beauty in a section of the state of New York intimately associated with the romance and terror of Indian warfare. He was of a vigorous, pugnacious and aggressive nature; he heard stories of adventure from Indian fighters and trappers, for the frontier had only recently been moved westward. He was sent to Yale College, but his temperament led him into acts of insubordination which prematurely ended his career as a student; and he went to sea in further pursuit of adventure. After varied experiences, valuable chiefly because they furnished him with material for several sea stories, two of which — "The Pilot" and "The Red Rover" — are still widely read, he came ashore, married and made his home in the city of New York.

His first venture in fiction was a dull story of English society life, which he knew only by hearsay. But "Precaution," which might well have died of its name, was succeeded and obliterated the following year by "The Spy." The earlier tale was in the mood of Provincial America, not yet aware of its own resources; the second tale was a story of the country lying across the river from New York and of the heroic days still remembered by many of Cooper's contemporaries. It was a stirring tale of the border warfare between the patriots and the Tories — as the adherents of the British government were called by the rebellious Americans; it described events of high interest in a history which Americans were already idealizing, and it con-

SECTIONAL LITERATURE

tained a strongly drawn character, Harvey Birch, the spy, which appealed to the imagination and patriotism of the country. "The Spy" may be said to have leaped into popularity both at home and abroad. It was translated into many languages, and a year after Cooper's death a writer on Nicaragua declared that it was the best-known book in English in South America; he found it everywhere.

"The Spy" was the first story of American life by an American, of permanent literary value and significance; but other stories as distinctively of the soil were to follow and surpass it in popular interest. In Indian habits, manners and character, which Cooper knew at first hand, he had material which was not only new but novel. Europe was intensely curious about the Indian; from the time of the earliest discoveries strange and terrifying tales of his cunning and cruelty had passed from country to country; and in America he was still a menace, a savage and merciless foe or an idle drunken loafer. The five novels of the Leatherstocking Series were novels of adventure which had the significance

AMERICAN IDEALS

of history as well as the interest of fiction. For the first time the Indian was sympathetically presented and the romance of frontier life reduced to terms of literature, so to speak. For the trapper and the pioneer played almost as great a part as the Indian in these tales. Leatherstocking is, indeed, Cooper's most vital creation; the lonely figure on the advancing line of civilization, a child of the old order freed from conventions by companionship with Nature; the pioneer who explored the forests, sailed over the great lakes, crossed the almost illimitable prairies and plains, from the boundaries of the original colonies on the seaboard to the ultimate limits of the continent on the western sea.

Cooper's style had neither flexibility nor variety; he was a careless writer, almost devoid of the finer qualities of the artist; he was diffuse and often commonplace, and he had little skill in portraiture. But he had the qualities demanded by his subjects: rapid narrative, graphic description, skill in keeping his readers in suspense, and genuine feeling for large effects on land and sea.

SECTIONAL LITERATURE

Cooper was an effective writer; Poe was preëminently the artist, interested neither in public movements nor in private morals, but in beauty, and in the workmanship which reflects and expresses it. The grandson of a soldier of the Revolution, Poe was the first Southern writer to make a lasting contribution to American literature; there had been other prose and verse writers of merit in that section, but they were of secondary importance. The interest of the South was in politics and oratory; fields in which the section long held a commanding position. Slavery was a feudal institution; the growing sentiment of the world put the South on the defensive; the section drifted out of the current of world movement; as a distinguished Southern writer of to-day has said: "Assuming provincialism to be localism, or being on one side or apart from the general movement of contemporary life, the South was provincial." Active out-of-door habits of life, a population devoted largely to agriculture, and a native aptitude for politics retarded literary expression among a people who had both the temperament and the love of action which play so great a part in poetry and in fiction.

Poe was the victim of an unhappy temperament and, while he found friends and opportunity in the crises in his career, he could neither keep the one nor make effective use of the other. His uncertain will, his unsettled habits, the many interruptions to his work, must be taken into account in any estimate of his production. He was a tireless and prolific writer; but, save in a little group of poems and of short stories, his genius never fully expressed itself. His life was in his work, for he was of a sensitive, highly strung nature, and the pursuit of beauty was a passion with him; and yet that work was essentially casual and fragmentary. It is well to remember, however, that an artist is under the compulsion of his temperament, and that the very qualities which limit and apparently defeat the largest expression of his genius often give his work its special distinction both of matter and of manner. Poe had a keenly analytic mind, but he was not a deep and fruitful thinker; he had exquisite artistic skill in construction, in dic-

SECTIONAL LITERATURE

tion, in the use of light and shade; but he lacked the broad and rich humanity of the great poets. His intelligence was clear and penetrating and took him far in the exploration of morbid temperaments; but it did not take him to the sources of poetic vitality, of great human qualities, of that abounding humor which is the overflow of a rich, wholesome nature. Poe was inventive rather than creative; he devised stories of fascinating intellectual ingenuity in which he played with his readers as if a chessboard were between them; he knew terror and mystery, and he had almost magical skill in taking possession not only of the imagination but of the senses of his readers. He was a magician rather than a man of creative genius; he stood outside his work; a pathetic spectral man of genius pursuing a substance which somehow changed to shadow when he overtook it.

Poe's distinction lies in the fact that he was preëminently the artist among American writers of his time; that he wrote a few lyrics of exquisite beauty; that he created a new kind of writing in what is called the story of Ratiocination; that he made the short story a work of art; and that, both by his exposition of literary principles and his criticism of the work of the writers of his time, he raised the standards and defined the methods of the art of writing. "The Murders in the Rue Morgue," "The Purloined Letter" and "The Gold Bug" have a European reputation; and, with "The Pit and the Pendulum," "William Wilson," "Ligeia," "The Fall of the House of Usher" and other tales of mystery and horror, and "Israfel," "Al Aaraaf," "The Haunted Palace," "Lines to Helen," "The City in the Sea" and other poems of magical euphonic beauty, have given Poe a distinctive influence in French and German literature.

In these writers, who may stand as representatives of a large group, New England, New York and the Middle Colonies and the South recorded their local traits, temperament, convictions. They are the voices of Sectional America; dealing with many things which were common to men of all parts of

SECTIONAL LITERATURE

the country, but speaking from the sectional consciousness. There have always been men in America who have foreseen its development, and in the days of the struggling colonies predicted the coming nation; and more than once in Emerson, in Lowell, in Whittier, one heard the vibration of the national note; but the note of prophecy lacks the resonance, the fullness of tone, the vibrating quality of the note of fulfillment.

The nation was born in the throes of the four years' War between the States; a struggle of tremendous forces waged with equal determination and patriotic devotion by both contestants. The question of the extension of the system of slavery into the newer States disappeared as the struggle deepened in the consciousness of the people into a conflict between two opposing views of the structure of the government. Was it a voluntary association of sovereign States dissoluble at will, or was it a Nation?

Each year on memorial days the men who fought in both armies march in thinning ranks through great crowds, hushed into silence or breaking into cheers as they pass; but already the old antagonisms are buried, and a nation has come out of the storm and anguish of those years. But what has been happily called a moral miracle of reconciliation does not blur the agony of those years, the haunting sense of peril to things as dear as life and to persons far dearer, the exhausting drain on the resources of the country, the heart-breaking suspense.

In these soul-searching experiences a nation was born. The practical work went on, as such work must go on, in the very throes of revolution, but the country waited at times with bated breath for news from the battle-fields, and all other interests waited on the course of events. Spirited lyrics were written on both sides, and the nation came out of the struggle with three or four songs which gave expression to deep feeling or passionate devotion to both causes. Of these the most impressive is "The Battle Hymn of the Republic"; the most poetic in phrase and feeling is "Maryland, My Maryland"; while the most "catching," to use a word which carries with it a

SECTIONAL LITERATURE

sense of immediate appeal easy to remember and of singable rhythm, is "Dixie," the popular Confederate song, which Mr. Lincoln, in a speech from the porch of the White House a few nights before his death, humorously said the nation had acquired by conquest. "The Star-Spangled Banner," the national anthem, is neither poetic in diction nor easily singable by crowds of people, and Americans still wait for a national hymn which shall be at once noble and simple.

VI

NATIONAL LITERATURE

THE War between the States not only made the power of the Federal government supreme and the union of States indissoluble, but it defined the national idea in terms which the whole country understood. There was no breaking down of State lines; they are as definite as they were before the struggle; but the States are no longer sovereign; they are integral and inviolable parts of a larger sovereignty. There will always be differences of opinion with regard to the proper division of authority between the States and the nation; but the fundamental question of supreme authority has been settled forever. Americans who used to consider questions of policy from the standpoint of their several States now consider such questions from the standpoint of the nation; and those who used to think in terms of a section now think in terms of a continent.

NATIONAL LITERATURE

In the making of a nation there must be means of free intercourse between different sections and free interchange of information and ideas. One of the most competent students of American life, M. Brunetière, the distinguished critic and editor of the *Revue de Deux Mondes*, as the result of a journey of observation across the continent, expressed his conviction that one of the most serious obstacles to the development of the higher civilization in America is the distance between the leading cities. New Orleans, for instance, is 1400 miles distant from Boston, Chicago 1100 miles from Washington, and San Francisco 3000 miles from New York. These great distances between sections would have been almost insuperable obstacles to the growth of a vital unity of opinion, feeling and action between the East and the West if they had not been diminished by modern methods of communication. In the days of the stagecoach and the canal, a self-governing nation of continental magnitude would have been impossible. The divergence of political ideas and feeling between the North and the

AMERICAN IDEALS

South was greatly intensified by the ignorance of each section of the point of view and habits of thought of the other. The War between the States created a nation; transcontinental lines of railroads, habitual use of the telegraph, the introduction of the telephone, mailing facilities, furnished the instrumentalities which annihilated distance, obliterated time and made the continent workable. And in recent years the area of neighborhoods has been greatly extended by trolley lines, automobiles, bicycles, the rural delivery of the mails.

Americans possess their continent in every part, not only by residence, but by the habit of travel. They make long journeys on the shortest notice and as a matter of course. Every week Americans travel 550,000,000 miles on railroads, and every year they spend $564,000,000 on railroad tickets. The automobile, which began its career as the toy of the very rich, has been speedily democratized, and its uses for rapid communication between localities and for local delivery have been developed to such an extent that it is as

NATIONAL LITERATURE

much a part of the general system of communication as the railroad or the steamboat. In brief, for purposes of travel, the continent is no larger than was New England fifty years ago; and for purposes of communication of knowledge and ideas it has become a neighborhood.

Sectional America expressed its mind and revealed its spirit in a literature which, while not of the first importance judged by universal standards, revealed talent of a high order and a rich content of varied experience; what has National America achieved in the field of spiritual and artistic expression and in what degree does its internal commerce of thought rival its commercial development and unify the many minds of its people? At the close of the war two poets of strikingly contrasted ideals and conditions began to make themselves heard. Many of the older poets were still writing, and the tradition of the New England group and of Poe had established, not only a standard of workmanship, but had identified poetry in the mind of the country with certain principles of selection of subjects proper for poetic treatment, and with a dignity of manner which had acquired a professional authority.

The appearance of Walt Whitman gave the literary proprieties a distinct shock, and, as often happens in the case of men whose genius is in excess of their training and taste, his eccentricities attracted the attention of the many, while his imagination, which had a quality new in American literature, was recognized by few. To the sharp criticism of his neglect of form and his lack of reticence — much of which was eminently sound and just — Whitman was indifferent. He was without social or educational background; he had never been in a university atmosphere; literary and social traditions did not exist for him; what had been said and the way in which it had been said were matters of indifference to him; his only concern was to give free expression of his own personality. With nonchalant ease he began with the declaration "I celebrate myself," and this celebration went on to the day of his death. He was the son of a mechanic, lived in the neighborhood

NATIONAL LITERATURE

of New York, attended the public schools, read novels omnivorously, and also the English Bible, Shakespeare, Ossian and such translations as came his way of the Greek tragedies, the Nibelungenlied, Dante and a few Oriental poems. He had little formal training, but acquaintance with some of the masters of universal literature. He lived not far from the sea and early felt its fascination.

He loved association with men of primitive vigor and habits, and comradeship was his habit as well as his social ideal. He spent much time in the streets, and on the ferries that then, in great numbers, crossed the two rivers between which the city of New York lies; he became a printer and journalist and combined both occupations with a roving disposition; he learned at first hand the working people in many parts of the country. During the war he served as a volunteer army nurse, and endeared himself to many men in the ranks by his gentleness, patience and the quality of comradeship to which he gave so much space in his verse. Impaired health made active work impossible, and Whitman's closing years were spent in busy idleness; he was cared for by devoted friends, writing when the mood seized him, discussing his contemporaries and their work with great freedom, and showing himself on occasions of literary interest. His disciples were few in numbers, but of an aggressive spirit of devotion; the country at large recognizes his genius, but has never taken him to its heart.

The fundamental thought in his work is his conception of Democracy as a vast brotherhood, in which all men are on an equality, irrespective of individual traits and qualities. There is nothing finer in him than his passion for comradeship; in his idealization of the fellowship between man and man he not only sounded some sincere notes, but he struck out some great lines in the heat of a feeling which seems always to have had quick access to his imagination. To this all-embracing affection, so deeply rooted in his conception of the democratic order, he devotes a large group of poems. His friends of the spirit were not chosen by any principle of taste; they are chiefly "powerful uneducated persons."

NATIONAL LITERATURE

It cannot be said with justice that Whitman erases all moral distinctions and rejects entirely the scale of spiritual values; but it is quite certain that he blurs them, and reduces his world to unity by putting aside the principle of selection. His underlying religious conception of life is essentially Oriental, and dates back to the time before the idea of personality had been clearly grasped. This conception Whitman does not consistently apply, for he lays tremendous emphasis on "powerful uneducated persons"; but it is wrought into his presentation of the democratic order of society.

Whitman was a pathfinder, and his joy in the new world of human experience he explored no one would take from him. It will be seen some day that there was a true prophetic strain in him; and that he marked the beginning, not of a new kind of literature, but of a new and national stage of literary development in America. In his verse the sections disappear and the Nation comes into view; the provinces fade and the continent defines itself. It is man at work over a continent that stirs him; he celebrates few persons; Lincoln alone seems to have moved him profoundly; even when he celebrates himself, it is as an incarnation and embodiment of human qualities and experiences.

While Whitman was making a system out of the confused movement of Democracy, Sidney Lanier, in life and in verse, was giving the old-time quality of distinction fresh and modern illustration. A Southerner by birth; of gentle breeding; a student at a small local college; a soldier in the Confederate army; captured and imprisoned by the Federal troops; released without resources and walking the long distance to his home; trying the occupations of clerk and teacher in a vain search for his vocation; happily married to a woman who gave him the sustaining comradeship of complete understanding and devotion; early developing pulmonary weakness and fighting for his life with indomitable patience and desperate courage,—Lanier found at last, in the Johns Hopkins University, opportunities of study and of work. He was an accomplished musician in the theory as

NATIONAL LITERATURE

well as in the practice of the art, and he became an expert in knowledge of English literature, especially of the early texts. An appointment as lecturer in English at the University gave him financial support and more leisure for writing. In his "Science of English Verse" the thoroughness of his methods and the great importance he attached to music, in the technical sense, in versification, were clearly shown. His passion for music and his conviction that it furnished the key to English verse seriously affected the spontaneity and natural melody of his own poetry. His technical knowledge gave his verse at times an intellectual rather than a verbal perfection, and only in a few pieces does his genius find free and musical expression.

For he had genius of a kind which was new in American poetry. Other poets had invested the aspects of the seasons, the forms of work in the fields, seedtime and harvest, with poetic significance; Lanier had the sense of the deep, moving life of things, of the faint stirrings of growth individually inaudible but collectively musical, of the arching sky

AMERICAN IDEALS

which sends across the marshes waves of color, and of the atmosphere in which the soul of a landscape seems to brood over it. The group of poems called "The Marshes of Glynn" are in curious contrast with New England poetry. The solitude and mystery of those moving stretches of live-oaks, swaying grasses, murmuring leaves,

> "low couched along the sea,"

are inviolable, and yet they seem, in the poet's vision, like a beautiful, many colored parable of human condition and destiny. In his song of the "Corn" the vital processes of nature are notated, so to speak, with a penetration which searches their very roots in the secrecy of mother earth, and registers, in the same moment, the long, slow waves of sound which sweep over great fields when the winds pass. Lanier said of Poe that he knew too little; it may be said of Lanier that he knew too much. His knowledge sometimes handicapped his spontaneity; and his verse became scientific in its precision of statement. But he died young; he had very noble qualities of nature and of mind, and he must be

NATIONAL LITERATURE

counted one of the most original American poets.

In Whitman and Lanier one is aware of a larger movement of imagination, a new-world air of freedom and space. The most obvious fact in the history of American writing since National America was born is the extension of literary interest and expression. The working and publishing centers for writers, as for artists, are still Boston and New York; but the whole continent makes contributions of books and pictures to these centers of distribution. In the field of fiction especially there has come into being a series of studies — a national *comédie humaine* — as comprehensive of local character and as rich in variety of temperament and habit as the nation.

The writing of the Provincial Period, which lasted until the appearance of Irving, Longfellow and Bryant, was crude in form and imitative in spirit; that of the Sectional Period, which lasted from about 1820 to the close of the War between the States in 1865, was on a high plane of workmanship and breathed a lofty spirit of independence and faith in human endeavor. But it was largely under the influence of English tradition and example; it was the literature of a people setting out boldly and confidently to try the experiment of Democracy, but with, as yet, little conception of the magnitude of the task; a people with the high aspiration, the entire self-confidence, the proud and sometimes insolent consciousness of strength, which are characteristics of youth. The Nation had an abiding faith in its destiny, but it had not taken possession of the continent, it had not faced the problems of a complex and swiftly developing prosperity and of the sudden influx of races bred under radically different conditions: in a word, the literature of Sectional America was the literature of a people which had not yet found itself.

Since the close of the war which established the Nation as the supreme political power, the American people have been coming to self-realization through knowledge of their history and through recognition of the grave problems which confront them. One of the striking facts in the American life of the last forty years

NATIONAL LITERATURE

has been the growth of the historical spirit and the widespread interest in the beginnings of the Nation. A historical literature of lasting value had come into existence during the Sectional period; but it is significant that, with a single notable exception, it dealt with foreign subjects. In point of style it had great charm, because it was the work of men of literary rather than of scientific or archæological training. Irving's residence in Spain bore fruit in an account of "The Conquest of Granada," the "Voyages and Discoveries of Columbus" and in the "Legends of The Conquest of Spain," conceived in the romantic spirit and written in a picturesque style. His biographies of Columbus, of Mahomet, of Goldsmith and of Washington are delightful footnotes to history. Prescott, a man of winning personality, whose blindness gave his work a heroic quality, was also drawn to subjects of romantic interest and told the story of the reign of "Ferdinand and Isabella," of "The Conquest of Mexico" and of Peru with the vivid interest of a novelist. Motley, a diplomatist and scholar, found themes congenial to Americans in the heroic age of the Dutch Republic and the United Netherlands; Bancroft, who also had experience as a diplomatist, wrote the first elaborate history of the United States in ten volumes; a work based on patient research, but written in a provincial style.

It was reserved for Parkman, a half-blind scholar and a lover of roses, to sketch with vigorous and picturesque hand the local background of American history in his account of Indian life and organization, and his brilliant story of the struggle between England and France for supremacy in America; a struggle as momentous in its consequences as the War of the Revolution and possibly of more decisive importance.

Americans had been too busy dealing with the present and making ready for the future to pay much attention to the past, and many parts of the country were without a past. But the War between the States definitely marked the end of an era, and closed a long chapter in the development of the country. Americans had talked heroically of their

NATIONAL LITERATURE

struggles; now they turned to a more serious study of their experiences with a desire to formulate the principles on which they had acted, often instinctively, and to understand what had been achieved and how it had been accomplished. Local history, which had been neglected save in a few localities, began to be studied with zeal; historical sites were marked by monuments; historical societies were organized in all parts of the country; and the teaching of history in the universities, which had been largely formal and of minor importance in the scheme of study, became a major subject; departments took the place of the single professor, and research work the place of instruction from textbooks. In the universities of the Central West the investigation of local origins was prosecuted with enthusiasm; on the Pacific coast the early Spanish records were rescued and put in shape for future historians; in the Johns Hopkins University laboratory methods were used to construct contemporary history by the study of magazines and newspapers.

The popular study of history has been

AMERICAN IDEALS

carried on, not only in the public schools, but by clubs in all parts of the country, by lectures, by public commemorations of historical events and anniversaries, by historical pageants, often of artistic merit. Meanwhile the libraries have been enriched by many historical works of value; studies of aspects of American history, of epochs, of administrations, of wars, of pioneering and settlement; of States, towns, counties and villages; and half-a-dozen histories of the United States have told the story for students and for popular reading as well. Schouler, McMaster, Adams, Rhodes, Fiske, have written the history of the United States from different points of view, and a large group of scholars have reënforced these broader surveys by studies of narrower scope but of lasting importance; and the footnotes to this national work in history in the form of biography have been almost numberless.

In this new interest in the beginnings of the nation the present was not overlooked; on the contrary, there appeared in different parts of the country, almost simultaneously, a group of writers of fiction who brought the

NATIONAL LITERATURE

short story to a perfection of form and of style not surpassed in any other literature. In character drawing, in the delicate art of sketching a background which has a vital relation to the story, in beauty of diction, many of these stories belong not only to American but to universal literature. Much has been said in America about "the great American novel"; the story that shall put between covers the very life of the nation in dramatic terms. That novel will never be written, because it is impossible to write it. "Vanity Fair" is a work of genius, but only a little section of English society gets into it, and the nation is mute in its pages. "Père Goriot" is also a masterpiece, but it is not even French in a large sense; it is Parisian. Tolstoi's "War and Peace" comes nearer being a great national novel, but it is already the story of a past age and of a Russia which has passed through radical changes. In a society in such different stages of development as the American, and affected by such a great variety of local conditions, a novel which shall present the form and substance of

AMERICAN IDEALS

the nation's character and manners is obviously beyond the range of possibility; this all-inclusive story demands the scope of a *comédie humaine.* Such a vital report of the form and color of their life Americans possess in their short stories, in which, although their literature still lacks the years of a full century, they have produced work of the highest quality.

There had been writers of fiction in the South before Poe wrote his stories of mystery; but he first showed a high degree of artistic power, and of their kind these stories remain unsurpassed; but Poe was not of a locality, not even of a nation; his imagination created its own world and his figures are visionary and spectral; they are like disembodied spirits. There is no part of America in which men and women are less elusive and generic and more human and individualistic than in the South; a section in which the code of honor has been held at times in higher respect than the law, and sentiment and feeling had far more appeal than reason.

Life on the plantations supplied a large

margin of leisure, respect for women became a cult as in the days of chivalry, but had its root in absolute purity of sex relations; and purity and leisure created an atmosphere of romance which blurred the hard outlines of slavery with a luminous mist. The open door, the open hand, and formality of manner tempered with winning cordiality, invested the old southern society with great charm. When the present generation of southern writers appeared on the stage, this social order had become a thing of the past, but it was still visible in a soft sunset light. In such stories as "Meh Lady" and "Mars Chan," by Mr. Page, a Virginian, this vanished society lives again in sentiment and ideal; while the Virginian moving across the mountains and becoming a frontiersman in Kentucky reappears in the beautiful art of Mr. James Lane Allen. In the farther South the naïve local elegance of the French manner, become captivatingly quaint in the French quarter in New Orleans where the Mississippi flows into the Gulf of Mexico, is to be found in Mr. Cable's "Old Creole Days," and "Madam Delphine."

AMERICAN IDEALS

Georgia, a state of more primitive types, has furnished homely humor and strongly marked types of native character to fiction; and Joel Chandler Harris, coming on the scene while the negro folk tales were still told to children, made "Uncle Remus" as famous in America as Rip Van Winkle; and the stories of the inimitable humor, pathos and cunning of the slave put into the mouth of this old negro form, perhaps, the most original American contribution not only to the literature of the last two decades, but to folklore as well. The mountaineers of Tennessee have been drawn against their striking mountain background by Miss Murfree and Mr. Fox.

Very early in this period Bret Harte wrote the rough romance of the mining camp with a fresh unconventionality and an energy of imagination which made certain kinds of frontier life familiar to the Nation. Samuel Clemens, better known as "Mark Twain," in his first and most original books, "Huckleberry Finn," "Tom Sawyer" and "Life on the Mississippi," portrayed life on the great river with a vital art and overflowing humor only temporarily eclipsed by his more popular but less original later work. The Far West of yesterday was fortunately seen in the last days of the grazing age by Mr. Wister, who has reported it with zest and sympathy; and, avoiding the melodramatic, has drawn the cowboy with his elemental virtues and vices. The vigor of the Central West, unconventional but overflowing with helpfulness and humor, radically democratic in spirit and optimistic in temper, has found capable recorders in Mr. Garland, Mr. Herrick and other novelists.

In New England there has been a report of the various types of character and of changing social and personal ideals of such vitality and charm as to worthily supplement the work of the earlier writers of this section. Miss Jewett by her quiet humor, her unobtrusive gift for character drawing and the refinement of her style, has become an American classic. Mrs. Mary Wilkins Freeman has reported New England individualism in terms of modern character with realistic skill relieved by humor.

In the cosmopolitan field Mr. James has written the short story with subtilty of insight, and Mr. Howells, his contemporary, with less elaboration of manner and more kindly and pervasive humor, has reported the foibles of one type of American woman with delightful skill.

The short story, while as exacting in its demands on the writer as the novel, imposes limitations of material and of manner from which the novelist escapes; and the painter of the major motives of American life needs a large canvas. Between Hawthorne and Mr. Howells there was a vast production of mediocre novels, with one notable exception; Mrs. Stowe wrote "Uncle Tom's Cabin" at white heat; she was a woman of vivid imagination, of eloquent and flowing style and of strong convictions, but she was very imperfectly trained in her art. The novel was a picture, and not a distorted picture, of slavery in its kindly patriarchal and its harsh industrial aspects. The anti-slavery agitation was becoming widespread; bitter feeling had been engendered and "Uncle Tom's Cabin" came at the psychological moment and intensified the feeling. The strikingly dramatic

NATIONAL LITERATURE

treatment of the very human material out of which the story was made, the intensity of feeling which imparted to it the driving force of a great passion, gave the story currency not only in America but in nearly all the languages of Europe; and until Mark Twain's books appeared no American book was so widely read.

Mrs. Stowe's novel was carried into popularity by the momentum of a great reform as well as by its own force; but it was not a work of art; on the contrary, it was marred by much crudity of form. The early work of Mr. Howells and Mr. James, on the other hand, was delightfully artistic. Both were men of modern education; interested in modern rather than in the classic literatures in which the earlier writers had been trained; and both were concerned with American life in its contemporaneous aspects. Mr. Howells has sketched, with a light hand and with kindly humor, the manners and ways of the American woman of the very feminine type; but he has also, in "The Rise of Silas Lapham," painted the portrait of the self-made man, of whom there are so many in America.

Mr. James lived in London for many years and saw his fellow countrymen, and especially his fellow countrywomen, against a background which threw their ways of thinking, of acting and of speaking into very effective relief. He belongs to a family which has won distinction in philosophy and the psychological interest of his stories has of late obscured their dramatic interest. He has, however, a rare talent for characterization and he is a master of the more subtle uses of language. He has distinction of manner rather than the grand manner, and his large canvases are painted with the refinement of cabinet pieces.

There are in America to-day a number of novelists of high attainment as artists and there are more whose work is stamped by vitality and force rather than by skill. The older and more conventional society of the East has found in such novels as "The House of Mirth" studies of that small subdivision popularly known as "the Smart Set" of a

NATIONAL LITERATURE

veracity so minute and unsparing as to produce the effect of satire; while stories of a broader outlook and of a freer manner, like "The Awakening of Helena Richie" and "The Iron Woman," have dramatized the problems of human experience with vital skill. The afterglow of earlier and local social ideals in a small community is reflected in the pages of Mr. Wister's "Lady Baltimore"; and the broad humor, the elemental passions, the full-blooded and unashamed humanity of the frontier, in his story of far-western life, "The Virginian." In a novel of Kansas life, "A Certain Rich Man," the biography, not only of a pioneer but of a community, may be read.

Stories of adventure are still written by Americans in great numbers, but the heroes of these tales are engineers, miners, railroad builders and organizers of great enterprises; and for the last two decades the human aspects of what is called "big business" have received increasing attention from novelists. In a series of three novels, only two of which were finished before his death, Frank Norris set out to write in terms of human experience the epic of wheat; its production in the vast fields of the Southwest, its passage through the vortex of the exchange in Chicago, its distribution to the far ends of the earth. In the hands of a young man the effort was premature, but it was significant of the present tendency in fiction to dramatize the tremendous forces evoked by American conditions, their reaction on character and life, and the problems they have created.

Americans are much given to the reading of fiction, and novels are manufactured in large quantities by facile writers to meet the popular demand. These stories are, as a rule, morally clean, and they are not devoid of invention and dramatic situation; but they are imitative and crude and have no place in any account of American literature.

The passing of the older group of poets was coincident with great changes in the national life; a wave of unprecedented prosperity rolled over the country, vast enterprises were projected and carried through, the engineer and the financier became the most prominent

NATIONAL LITERATURE

figures in the arena. Education took a practical turn, technical and trade schools multiplied, and scientific education began to lead literary education in popular interest. The war with Spain for the liberation of Cuba, with the unforeseen appearance of the American flag in the Far East, stirred the imagination of the Nation, not with dreams of conquest or with military ambition, but with a sense of national solidarity and of national responsibilities. Without surrendering the policy of avoiding entanglements with other nations and keeping out of the circle of international politics in the Old World, defined by Washington, the Nation awoke to the consciousness of world-wide relations and of the responsibilities which came with such relations. The enormous development of business and the rapid accumulation of capital created problems new to American life.

Meantime the whole world was moving with dramatic rapidity. Japan had taken her place on the stage of world activity with startling suddenness, and in her brilliant achievements in arms and industry Americans were quick to see the dawn of a new day in the East, the emergence of influences and ideals which will temper and enrich western civilization. The story of humanity, told in serial form in the newspapers day by day, became of absorbing interest. The literature of economics, sociology, government, politics, reform grew rapidly to large proportions, and for the time being books of knowledge, of political and social philosophy, hold the attention of the Nation and books of purely literary quality are given less prominence. This does not mean that Americans are losing their inherited idealism; for the movements which are fast realigning political parties in the United States express the growing determination to bring both politics and business into greater harmony with political and social ideals.

Poetry, meantime, has less vogue; largely, it may be suspected, because few poets have not yet spoken with compelling power the words the people are longing to hear. In the generation which followed the War between the States there was a group of poets whose

NATIONAL LITERATURE

feeling for artistic qualities was keener than their predecessors; a great reform had been carried to completion and a period of ethical relaxation and ease of mood followed. Of this period perhaps the country will remember longest Thomas Bailey Aldrich, a poet whom the French would have called a "little master," so exquisite was his craftsmanship, so delicate his art. Mr. Moody, Mr. Woodberry and Dr. Van Dyke have enriched American poetry with work of lasting charm and vitality.

Other poets there were, bred under academic influence, whose work has notable beauty but lacks the appeal to the popular imagination. In the youngest generation of poets now beginning to make themselves heard new phases of life appear; often presented, it is true, in the harsh phrase of the reformer, but indicative of a shifting of interest from classical and traditional themes to the human needs and aspirations of to-day. The themes of poetry are rarely wholly new, but the deepening passion for social justice finds expression in protest against inhuman conditions of life and work, and in dramatic appeals for a larger regard for the welfare of the workers. American poetry has always been idealistic, and has interpreted national opportunity in terms of spiritual and moral responsibility; to-day it has become altruistic and its themes are justice for the worker, international peace and human brotherhood. This newer poetry has yet to prove its claims to be heard by the manner as well as the matter of its message; but it is full of promise. The vigorous recent production of poetic plays may be characterized in the same words. Since the days of Irving the essay has been a form of literature congenial to the American type of mind. Emerson, Lowell, Holmes, Thoreau, Curtis used it as a medium for criticism, for informal philosophy, for ethical and social teaching. Its best traditions of sanity of thought, humor and soundness of forms are continued to-day in the work of Mr. Burroughs, of Messrs. Bliss Perry, Frank Colby, Brander Matthews, Henry D. Sedgwick, Dr. Van Dyke and Dr. Crothers and others. In power of analysis and intellectual force and integrity Mr. Brownell's critical essays

NATIONAL LITERATURE

hold a place by themselves in American writing.

Of the many names mentioned in this survey of American literature as an expression of the American life only half a dozen have world-wide range: Cooper, Poe, Emerson, Whitman, Mark Twain. The great body of contributors to the national literature are known only in their own country. If one looks at literature as significant in the degree in which it produces masterpieces, the American must wait, as other peoples have waited, for a more complete fusion of the elements of national life and the broader and deeper national consciousness that will come with it. But if one consider literature as an expression of the soul of a people, American literature has already, less than a century from its birth, attained lasting significance. It is the spoken word of a people whose beginning was a great adventure, and whose life has been a great toil.

What have their books to tell us of their innermost thoughts? What sent them across the perilous seas and has kept them to their

AMERICAN IDEALS

tasks? Briefly these things: passion for liberty, sense of moral order and responsibility, faith in God and man, love of home and of Nature; and a habit of humor born of hope, of courage and of the good will of a community which has spread from ocean to ocean, but still keeps the neighborly feeling which makes the village, in time of calamity or of need, one family.

VII

THE AMERICAN IN ART

IN the pre-Revolutionary period there were churches that charmed the eye and conveyed a sense of their uses to the mind in Portsmouth, Newport, New York, Wilmington, Charleston; and there were houses which happily harmonized material and form, and were suggestive of social background and vistas of an older social order, in Salem, Boston, Providence, Bristol, Newport, New York, Philadelphia, Germantown, Annapolis, Richmond, Charleston, and smaller towns. Colonial architecture at its best suggested a good tradition and expressed an honest fact; it expressed history and a sound relation to the soil. It had that ultimate elegance, entire simplicity, which was characteristic of the best colonial life, and that dignity which was the stateliness of the Old modified by the conditions of the New World. The churches built under the inspiration of

AMERICAN IDEALS

Sir Christopher Wren, and the fine old homes, of which the Sherborne house in Portsmouth, the Jumel mansion in New York, and Mount Vernon, may serve as examples, bore the impress of a certain distinction of taste and form which were the heritage of the few, but of inestimable importance to the many, as examples of true American architecture. They were as vitally related to their surroundings as are the gray old great houses of England and the square-towered country churches to the low skies and deep foliage of the ripe and mellow landscape. They constituted, with the little group of buildings like Independence Hall in Philadelphia, a native order of building, adapted, it is true, but not imitative. They stood for Provincial America, with its face turned eastward, and still bound to Europe by kinship if not by identity of standards and interests.

Architectural chaos came much later, but the empire of the commonplace had been established in all parts of the country as early as 1840. American writers had been telling the truth for many years before

THE AMERICAN IN ART

later American builders began to do anything more radical than mumble a few commonplaces; when they started out to speak for themselves they made sad work of it. To begin with, they did not speak the truth; they were ungrammatical; worst of all, they were vulgar. During the period which followed the War between the States, which has been aptly called the reign of terror in American architecture, crimes against stone, wood, iron, and form of every kind were perpetrated, which still cry aloud for vengeance. It was in this period that post offices and other federal buildings were sown broadcast over a helpless land, and ugliness in almost unbroken monotony was set up as a symbol of public life. There were a few redeeming exceptions, but for the most part the state buildings of this period were monstrous offenses against public morals and public taste. This was the period, too, of the so-called reconstruction policy, which was a shocking parody of the sublime tragedy of the War; and it is significant that shining deeds of valor, and heroes whom youth and death

AMERICAN IDEALS

had touched with a double beauty, were commemorated at this time with monuments and statues, of many of which it is merciful to write that they were executed not in malice, but in ignorance. Never before, perhaps, has a great sacrifice found such meaningless expression in monumental form; and it will be the pious task of a later generation to raze many of these monuments to the ground, and worthily commemorate a sublime chapter of national history.

During this lawless period all sorts of hybrids were brought to birth, and many still remain to remind us of our mortality: houses so entirely made with hands that no suggestion of mind flows from them; Italian villas (pronounced with a long *I*); stone castles with colonial additions; Elizabethan mansions with late Victorian piazzas and verandas; structures of no order but with vast cupolas; and, worst of all, riotous variations of that shamefully abused Queen Anne house, which, in its proper form and place, has a real relation to domestic life and beauty of adaptation.

THE AMERICAN IN ART

There was admirable building in the colonial and sub-revolutionary period; then came the age of the commonplace and the monotonously undistinguished; to be followed, after a great national crisis, by an outbreak of self-assertion, which was anarchistic in its wild and truculent disregard of authority, principle and law; a flamboyant declaration of the right of the free American citizen to make his country as ugly as he chose; a riot of ignorance, bad taste, extravagance, and crude independence.

It must not be forgotten, however, that in the darkest days of marble palaces with painted iron columns, and of bastard Queen Anne cottages rising sanguinary and ostentatious above diminutive lawns, builders who were also architects, or architects who were also builders, as in the "elder days of art," were patiently trying to persuade their clients that building was an ancient art and not a local job; and that an increasing number of those who were teachable in these matters made life tolerable in prosperous communities. The remnant of the elect increased not only

AMERICAN IDEALS

in knowledge, but in influence, and the statement by a well-known architect that American architecture was the "art of covering one thing with another to imitate a third thing, which, if genuine, would not be desirable," began to lose point. Upjohn, Renwick, Hunt, Richardson, Root, and White suggest a movement in education, and a genuine achievement in an art which more than any other ought to have in this country a hand as free as its opportunity is great. If vagaries are still seen in stone, wood, and iron, and if the ready adapter and servile imitator are still in the land, there are increasing evidences of the presence of the artist and of the patron who is wise enough to give him his chance.

American painting has passed through gray, uneventful years, but it has never known a reign of terror.

It is true, the earlier painters were English rather than American, and it is also true that they did not rank with the best; but the best, it ought to be remembered, were Reynolds and Gainsborough. Peale, Copley, and Stuart

THE AMERICAN IN ART

made places for themselves in the history not only of American, but of English, art, though their rank in the colonies was much higher than in the mother country. To them and to their pupils we owe not only a tradition of sound workmanship, but a large group of portraits which are of immense social and historic interest. They were the most graphic and vital historians of the older American society. It was inevitable that they should be English in taste and manner, since they were dealing almost entirely with English faces at a time when Americans were still Englishmen in new surroundings; the best service they could render to their contemporaries was to make them familiar with good work. Less fortunate artists who began by painting signs ended in several cases by painting good portraits and miniatures. John Wesley Jarvis, who was born in England and named after his famous uncle, was taken to Philadelphia at an early age, and received his education in the irregular manner of a country in which the value of art schools was a matter of remote future discussion. "In my school days," he writes, "the painters of Philadelphia were Clark, a miniature painter, and Galagher, a painter of portraits and signs; he was a German who, with his hat over one eye, was more *au fait* at walking Chestnut Street than at either face or sign painting. Then there was Jeremiah Paul, who painted better and would hop farther than any of them; another who painted red lions and black bears, as well as beaux and belles, was old Mr. Pratt, and the last that I remember of that day was Rutter, an honest sign-painter, who never pretended or aspired to paint the human face divine, except to hang on the outside of a house; these worthies, when work was plenty, flags and fire buckets in demand, used to work in partnership, and I, between school hours, worked for them all, delighted to have the command of a brush and a paint pot. Such was my introduction to the fine arts and their professors." Copley, West, Stuart, Peale, Trumbull, and Allston were court painters in ease of condition compared with some of their obscure fellow-craftsmen in the coun-

THE AMERICAN IN ART

try; and, taking into account their limitations of temperament, they were not unequal to their opportunities.

There were commonplace painters between the later pupils of West and the generation of Kensett, Whittredge, and Gifford; but neither during that period nor later was there a reign of terror in American painting; there was, on the contrary, a more or less steady gain in craftsmanship and originality. Whatever may have been the limitations of the group of gifted men who are popularly regarded as belonging to the Hudson River School, they were trained in good traditions, and they interpreted the landscape of the country for the first time with deep feeling and sympathetic knowledge. They were men of generous and enthusiastic nature, and the breadth and wildness of American scenery moved them to large artistic endeavors. Their work was done out of doors, in a spirit of resolute fidelity to what they saw, and with simplicity of method.

If the vastness of scale of American scenery appealed to Church and Bierstadt, its poetry

AMERICAN IDEALS

was felt by Inness, Martin, and Wyant, in whose work there was an individuality of insight and of expression which showed that the apprentice period in American painting was at an end, and the day of distinctive achievement at hand. Mr. Vedder reached his majority in 1857, and with him enters the element of mystery, the suggestion of fate, into American painting. There was nothing esoteric in his interpretations of figures and faces; no pretense on the part of the artist to the possession of a secret cipher, an occult knowledge, which his art implied but did not betray; on the contrary, its most potent suggestiveness is the feeling it conveys that the artist saw and painted something as essentially unknowable to him as to his most intelligent student. When the illustrations to the "Rubaiyat" appeared in 1887, Mr. Vedder's work was well known by a few lovers of art, but that vague and cold collective person, "the general public," successor of the "gentle reader," had no acquaintance with it. The suggestiveness and power of the pictorial interpretation of Omar Khay-

THE AMERICAN IN ART

yam deeply impressed the imagination of the country, not only because the manner was novel and the matter in striking contrast to the prevailing mood, but because the form was at once simple and fundamentally unified, and obviously and broadly beautified. The work was almost classical in its definiteness, but the richness of its texture, the solidity of its presentation, the liberal use of emblems and symbols, gave it a quality remote from familiar things, and kept the painter well in front of the philosopher. In the work of Mr. Vedder, as in that of Inness and Martin, the imagination began to move along original lines and to disclose a fresh and powerful impulse.

In 1862 William Morris Hunt settled in Boston, and began a career which was too short to fulfill the hopes it awakened. If there was something lacking in mastery of technique, there was, in "The Bathers," in "The Boy and the Butterfly," in the decorations which gave distinction to the Albany Capitol and were sacrificed, — as art always is when it is innocently involved in a political job,

AMERICAN IDEALS

— and in many of the portraits, a rich language of temperament, a luminousness, a command of tones full of ardor and passion, which revealed the presence of a genius trained in the Old but reveling in the freedom and audacity of the New World.

Whistler and La Farge came of age a little later, and, in very diverse ways, exhibited that happy coming together of genius and culture which precedes fertility of high-class work in all the arts, and which, in the case of these two painters, gave American painting secure place in the critical opinion of the world. The work of both craftsmen was saturated with feeling, with personality of rare quality, and irradiated again and again by the magic of inspiration. Mr. La Farge has so lately gone from us, but the completeness of the disclosure of his gifts in the comparatively small mass of his work makes it proper to speak of it as a rounded achievement. It may be said of him with safety, as of Whistler, that he has never sacrificed art to any kind of expediency, nor shaped his work to any passing interests; but with

THE AMERICAN IN ART

the unswerving fidelity of a man of deep artistic instincts, he served his country by regarding not what it craved, but what alone could finally satisfy it. The note of distinction in his work, as in that of Whistler and of a considerable group of younger painters, has been an immense consolation to those who have feared that the price for the obvious material comforts of democracy might be a loss of fineness of feeling, of a certain elevation, dignity and superiority of ideal and manner which have always been present in the greater achievements of art.

Whistler published the Normandy etchings in 1858; four or five years later his portraits of his mother and of Carlyle appeared, to be followed in the next decade by the incomparable etchings of Venice, of the Thames, of glimpses of the sea, of those odds and ends of buildings whose decay the twilight or the distance touched with a charm incommunicable by a hand less sensitive, subtle, and sure. Against an English background the audacity and brilliancy of Whistler's mind and temperament, his amazing skill in the

AMERICAN IDEALS

dialects of verbal warfare, the flash and sting of his repartee, were immensely heightened, and prove him the alien he always claimed to be. His skill in expression was little short of magical; and if, in the dispassionate judgment of his work by future generations, it shall seem to lack fundamental power, there can be no skepticism touching its beauty, subtlety, delicacy, — the specific qualities which many critics have agreed must perish under the blight of democracy.

American painting had ceased to be isolated and provincial long before the United States had been forced out of a seclusion from the affairs of the world, which it cherished as an historic policy after the conditions of modern civilization had entirely changed, and the endeavor to separate privilege from responsibility had become as futile as it was selfish. Men whose work bears the marks of locality as distinctly as that of Eastman Johnson and Winslow Homer; of personal idealism, ascending at times to the height of vision, as that of Fuller among the older, and Thayer among the younger, men; of brilliant and audacious character-reading and brushwork, as that of Sargent; of forceful or charming individuality of observation of nature and of the human face, as that of Tyron, Brown, Foster, Brush, Walker, Beckwith, Alexander, Cecilia Beaux, — to select a few among many representative names, — by a common sincerity of feeling, by great diversity of gifts, and by high seriousness of spirit, emancipated American painting from provincial tastes, local standards, and national complacency.

Fifty years ago, American sculpture was a matter of a few names, a few pieces of well-cut marble, and a considerable mass of pretty and meaningless reminiscences of Italian ateliers. Ignorance of the art was widespread, and where ignorance ended prejudice began. There was a chilling suspicion of the decency of sculpture, and the unhappy artist who hinted at the existence of the human form under clothes was regarded as a dealer in immorality. In Philadelphia, in 1845, a few casts from the antique created something very like a public scandal; and when, at an earlier period, Greenough's "Chanting Cherubs," the first group by an American sculptor, was exhibited, a storm of condemnation enveloped the undraped figures; nude babies were familiar in American homes, but their appearance in public shocked the moral sense of the whole community. This was in New York, where, in early times, gentlemen who profited by piracy had been influential members of society. The symbolism of Powers's "Greek Slave," and the passionate sympathy with the Greek struggle for freedom, diverted attention from the nudity of the figure to the pathos it expressed; but it was thought necessary, in the interests of public morals, that the fair captive should be examined by a committee of experts. Accordingly, a group of clergymen in Cincinnati sat as a jury and, after a critical examination of the figure, issued a kind of license for purposes of public exhibition. The humor of submitting the statue to the inspection of a committee of clergymen does not seem to have occurred to any save a few Americans who had been cor-

THE AMERICAN IN ART

rupted by familiarity with foreign galleries; nor does any one appear to have realized that the real immorality was not in the timid innocent slave, but in the public opinion which hailed her effigy as the greatest work of art in the history of the world.

These significant facts explain the eager haste with which Greenough, Powers, and Crawford fled to Italy and remained in that more genial clime. The sin of self-consciousness which made Americans blush when the human form was mentioned in polite conversation, the lack of public interest, the dense ignorance of public taste, and the absence of examples of the art and of fine marble, drove the little group of sculptors into lifelong exile. Houdon, the Frenchman, and Cerrachi, the Italian, had done some interesting work in this country; Rush and Augur had been timidly prophetic in wood and stone; there were Italian carvings in some of the colonial homes; but it was still very early dawn in American sculpture when Greenough, Powers, and Crawford became professional sculptors. Greenough and Crawford, despite the un-

AMERICAN IDEALS

evenness of their work and their partial success in large undertakings, made contributions of lasting artistic and historical value to the art which they practiced with passionate fidelity. Powers lacked temperament, vigor, the creative imagination; he never escaped the trammels of the Italian tradition and set his hand boldly and strongly to original work; but he carved some admirable portrait busts, full of character, firm in manner, and faithful in likeness.

How far the country had yet to go in understanding and appreciation of sculpture is brought out by the fact that in 1862 the National Congress commissioned a girl of fifteen, after an education in her art which lasted a twelvemonth, to execute a statue of Lincoln, which now stands in the rotunda of the Capitol at Washington, among other effigies of departed statesmen whose enforced absence alone secures the safety of the collection. In that melancholy hour the country was standing, however, on the threshold of that day of free and varied creativeness which has given contemporary American sculpture

THE AMERICAN IN ART

a place of the first importance in the interest of the artistic world. In no art was there for the first seventy years of the national life so little promise; in none has there been so great an achievement.

In 1857, Mr. Ward first modeled his Indian Hunter, which now stands, alert, alive, convincing, set low as if gliding through the shadows, in the foliage of New York's beautiful park. Eleven years later Saint Gaudens, whose death fell like a shadow over the awakening love of beauty in America, received the commission for the statue of Farragut, which put him at the forefront of American sculptors, and made an immediate impression on monumental art in the country. No figure set up in any public place in America has spoken with such simplicity and humanness of speech to the mighty tides that stream past it on the most crowded of American thoroughfares, nor has any more distinctly given a fresh and invigorating impulse to an art but lately emancipated from foreign influence and timidly venturing to give its soul play. The Lincoln in the Chicago Park which bears its name has been accepted as the foremost portrait statue in the New World; the beautiful and baffling figure in the Rock Creek Cemetery in Washington, clothed with majesty of the mystery of death; the Shaw Memorial in Boston, with its moving column of negro soldiers fast upon the leader who rides, young and immortal, into the ranks of the dead; and, finally, the superb Sherman Memorial at one of the entrances to Central Park, New York, held securely on its pedestal, but moving, invincible, and alive, like its great fellow in Venice: these are achievements to be reckoned with, not only as forming an inspiring chapter in the development of American sculpture, but as a lasting contribution to the art of the world. What a distance these works register from tentative work of the earlier sculptors; from Palmer's charming ideal heads, and those graceful figures which did so much to awaken popular interest in sculpture; from Ball's impressive monumental work; from the varied and cultivated creations of Story, that fascinating and many-

THE AMERICAN IN ART

sided American, whose life was so full of interest and occupation, and who was fluent in so many languages of art that nothing he accomplished quite expressed his vitality or fulfilled his promise!

The fine poise and noble serenity of Mr. French's work, in which the skill of the craftsman and the power of revealing beauty and strength to men untrained in art, are happily united; the virile audacity and boldness of Mr. Macmonnies; the striking and forceful originality of Mr. Barnard; Mr. Bartlett's "Lafayette," with its indefinable air of distinction, and his "Genius of Man" at the Pan-American Exposition; Mr. Boyle's "Stone Age," in Fairmount Park, Philadelphia; Mr. Adams's gracious and unfailingly fascinating portrait busts; Mr. Elwell's figures of "Ceres" and "Kronos" at the Buffalo Exposition; Mr. Ruckstuhl's strongly conceived "Spirit of the Confederacy"; Mr. Partridge's meditative study of Tennyson; Mr. MacNeil's "Sun Vow"; Mr. Lopez's "Sprinter"; Mr. Pratt's "Andersonville Prisoner Boy"; Mr. Dallin's "Signal of Peace"; Mr. Bringhurst's "Kiss of

Eternity"; Mr. Taft's "Solitude of the Soul" — to select a few representative works out of a great multitude — show how far the art of sculpture has gone in mastery of tools, courage of individual taste, variety and freshness of manner and subject, since the days when Greenough, Powers, Crawford, and Story found in Italy a refuge from the ignorance and indifference of their fellow countrymen.

The record of the progress of music has not been unlike that of sculpture. If it could be recalled in baldest outline, touching only its points of new departure, it would show the same general features. It was, for obvious reasons, more widely appreciated in the earlier times than sculpture, but its intelligent students were comparatively few, in spite of the fact that the old-fashioned schools for young women placed the study of music side by side with needlework, "elegant deportment and polite conversation." There was a great deal of that kind of music which Dumas called "the most expensive form of noise." A musical people could not and would not have accepted the "Star-Spangled

THE AMERICAN IN ART

Banner," with its terrible interrogatory "Oh, say," as a national anthem. There were homes, and even communities, in which singing and instrumental music were matters of taste and skill as well as of heart; but the country at large was a barren wilderness so far as the "concourse of sweet sounds" was concerned. To-day, in many large cities, it is impossible to make use of musical opportunities, so many and so interesting are they. In no art has there been so rapid and so wide a growth of intelligent interest during the last fifty years. In nearly all the large cities orchestras of thorough training are to be heard, and permanent organizations of highly educated musicians are fast becoming a feature of life in the large centers. New York has long been devoted to grand opera, and musical programs of every sort and kind are rendered to crowded audiences. It is true, all the other cities in the country are agreed that this musical interest is a fad, but it is equally true that it is so persistent and discriminating that it deceives the elect leaders of the Old World who conduct the

AMERICAN IDEALS

New York orchestras from time to time, and are deluded into the belief that the metropolis is a musical city. Boston listens, without impeachment of her intelligence, to her admirable orchestras, and educates an almost innumerable host of students in music. Philadelphia, Pittsburgh, Chicago, Cincinnati, have the most substantial claims to consideration as centers of interest in musical matters; while the growing enthusiasm for musical festivals in Worcester, Montclair, Bethlehem and other communities may be safely taken as indicative of a steadily widening area of knowledge and appreciation. Music is taught in some of the older colleges by teachers who are also composers, while in the young and vigorous institutions of the Central West the love of the art is a popular movement.

Side by side with an immense amount of vulgarity in sound, of hideous "ragtime" profanity, there is a growing critical sense in music. Stephen Foster's touch on the springs of emotion in "The Old Kentucky Home," "Old Folks at Home," "Nellie was

THE AMERICAN IN ART

a Lady," and other melodies which the whole continent sang or hummed sixty years ago, was a prelude to a very considerable production of popular music, lacking in classical quality, but with a certain naïve originality and significance in our musical development, as Dvorak was quick to see when he composed the New World Symphony. Such teachers as Professors Paine and Parker, who have been creators in the field in which they have long been conspicuous leaders in thoroughness of education; such composers as MacDowell, Chadwick, Hadley, Foote, Kelly, and Converse, and such conductors as Thomas, the elder Damrosch, Seidl, and Gericke, have brought Americans out of the desert of the mediocre and cheap in an art which has, perhaps more than any other, given freest and deepest expression to the modern temper and attitude, into a land of abundant and increasing fertility and refreshment.

VIII

SCHOOL AND COLLEGE

THE most eminent student of American life has said that the passion of the American is not for money, as many other observers have declared, but for education. The popular belief in its moral and political efficacy is a fundamental conviction and has developed an unprecedented generosity from legislatures and from private donors. Respect for scholarship came to America with the first settlers, though all the colonies did not attach the same importance to education. In England, Scotland and Holland the school, which had been the adjunct of the church and in a special sense the teacher of priests, did not cease to be religious when the Protestants came into power; on the contrary, they regarded education as their most important ally. When the people of Leyden, after one of the most heroic sieges in history, were offered by William of

SCHOOL AND COLLEGE

Orange perpetual remission of taxes, they asked that they might have a university; the Puritan movement in England was led largely by men who had studied at Cambridge, and the Puritan faith in education as the bulwark of religion went to New England with the earliest colonists and made that section a mother of colleges and a teacher of teachers.

The Virginia Company had no sooner set foot on the banks of the James River for commercial purposes than it set apart a large section of land for the use of a college to teach Indian children the rudiments of Christianity and of the Latin language, and money was collected in England to establish a school which should prepare children for this college. The failure of the company a few years later defeated these plans, but they reveal the mind of the men who were behind the enterprise. Conditions in Virginia were not favorable to popular education, but free schools were established here and there in the colony in the first half century of its history. Small private schools came into existence wherever there were groups of settlers; while the planters, who were becoming prosperous, provided private tutors for their children.

In New England preaching was a function of the very highest importance and preachers were leaders in public affairs; the education of preachers was, therefore, one of the matters to which the Puritan colonists gave earliest attention. They accepted the burden of supporting these schools as a public duty, and the maintenance of education by taxation became axiomatic while the feeble settlers were still fighting to keep standing-ground on the edge of the continent. In 1642, twenty-two years after the landing at Plymouth, Massachusetts ordained by law that every child should be taught "to read and understand the principles of religion and the capital laws of the country." This ordinance, narrow in conception but of immense capacity for future development, was the initial step in the evolution of the system of public education at public expense which has become one of the most characteristic features of American life. A little later, in the same

SCHOOL AND COLLEGE

section, every township, when it numbered fifty householders, was required to support a teacher; and towns numbering a hundred householders, to establish a school to teach Latin. These schools were often feeble and ineffective, but the little local schools with a single teacher traveled with the settlements. They were rude pioneer experiments, for the conditions which surrounded them were rude; their importance lay in the fact that they gave education a first place in public interest and accustomed people to think of education as a function of the community.

Nor did the interest of the colonist exhaust itself in establishing a rudimentary system of public education. In 1635, fifteen years after the landing of the first New England colony, the Boston Latin School was opened; an institution modeled after the English Grammar School, with which many of the colonists were familiar. This school remains to-day one of the best-known schools in America. Three years later, by the generosity of John Harvard, the first of the long line of American founders of colleges, Harvard College was opened for students; an institution which has long held a first place by reason, not so much of its age as of its success in training men of distinction, and its leadership in educational adaptation and experiment. Yale College, in the New Haven colony, was chartered in 1701; in 1691 a college had been established in Williamsburg, the capital of Virginia. William and Mary College owed its original endowment to private donors, to the English king and queen after whom it was named and who bestowed on it large tracts of unoccupied lands, and to the Virginia Assembly, which set apart for its support the proceeds of a specific import duty. But the college owed more to the stubborn determination of James Blair, a colonist from Scotland, than to any other person. He aroused the interest of the English sovereigns and of many prominent people in England in the proposed college. When he urged the need of it for the sake of the souls of the colonists on the Attorney-General, that important officer of the Crown said, irritably: "Damn your souls, make tobacco!" This

SCHOOL AND COLLEGE

sentence puts into a few forcible words the attitude towards the colonies which led to the disruption of their relations to the mother country. It was a picturesque statement of the colonial policy of the time when the use of colonies for revenue purposes was the chief concern of the home governments.

Virginia had a great share in the War of the Revolution and in the formation of the American government. In Washington she gave the colonists a leader who commanded their armies through the long and exhausting eight years' war, who became the first President and who remains the foremost American; and Thomas Jefferson, who drafted the Declaration of Independence, became the third President and defined the theory of the powers of the National government which has been held by one of the great political parties from the adoption of the Constitution. It is significant of the spirit of the founders of the American state that Washington, who had served through the war not only without compensation but paid his own expenses, made a generous bequest in his last will and testament for the founding of a national university; while Jefferson, who was strongly influenced by French thought, founded the University of Virginia in 1825. The other colleges, with the exception of Princeton, — which showed the influence of the Scotch universities, — were modeled largely on English college lines. The University of Virginia embodied French ideals and methods. It was distinctly a secular institution, while the other colleges were still more or less under the control of the different Christian churches, and their students received distinctive religious teaching in one form or another.

Education was not only a prime public interest in colonial America, but has become the chief interest in national America, which has moved steadily though often instinctively to the conviction that access to knowledge is not only a guarantee of popular government, but the supreme duty of such a government and the right of all its citizens. There is a national system of education in the United States, though there is no national control of education. In all the States education

SCHOOL AND COLLEGE

is provided for children at public expense; but the methods, extent and standards of this education are entirely within the control of the individual States. In a few States free education is not provided beyond the common school; in the majority of the States it is continued through the High School; in many States, especially in the West, it is continued through the university. The common school, open to all children everywhere, is the base of this system. In 1911 there were 17,813,853 pupils in such schools in the United States, and the forty-eight States paid for their support $426,250,434; a sum which exceeds one third of the annual expenditure of the National government, and more than doubles the expenditure of all the States for all other purposes; this sum being raised entirely by direct taxation on the localities which sustain the schools. These schools are under the general direction of local school boards elected by the voters of the district or of the town.

To these common schools supported by taxation must be added a multitude of schools supported by the various religious organizations, many of which are of high rank. The Roman Catholic Church has a widely extended system of parish schools in which more than a million children are taught. There are also several thousand schools conducted as private enterprises, often thoroughly equipped and beautifully housed. In many cities the kindergartens in the public schools are supplemented by kindergartens supported by individuals or by associations of private persons, who not only believe in the Froebelian ideas and methods of education for all young children but are convinced that the kindergarten is specially adapted to meet the needs of children in the congested quarters of large cities and in factory towns. The national government maintains a number of schools for Indian children, as a temporary expedient. And a large group of schools for negro children is supported by private means at points where the need of immediate education is pressing and the burden too heavy for local resources. Large gifts of land for educational purposes were made to the States when the

SCHOOL AND COLLEGE

National government had great unoccupied tracts at its disposal, and it maintains a Military Academy and a Naval Academy of high rank.

It will be seen that the National government does not support the educational system of the country because, in the division of functions, that function is discharged by the States. Within the last few years a National Bureau of Education has been established at Washington under the direction of the Commissioner of Education, but its work is not executive; it collects and formulates the statistics of education in all parts of the country and the information which it gathers and arranges is at the disposal of the country. The Commissioner is a non-political officer of the government and is chosen for his educational knowledge and executive ability. He has little direct authority but great influence, and that influence is likely to increase as the need of greater uniformity of standards and methods becomes more pressing with the extension of the school system.

AMERICAN IDEALS

A child in an American community which provides kindergartens enters the kindergarten at the age of four and the primary department of the common school of the district at six or seven. In this school he remains until his fourteenth year and is taught the rudiments — reading, writing, arithmetic, literature and science. In many schools provision is made for manual training and for the beginning of education in the trades. From his fourteenth to his eighteenth year, speaking generally, he is in the High School, where he pursues the same subjects in more advanced classes; adding to them, if he intends to go through college, special studies in the languages, history and science preparatory to his college work; or, if he proposes to enter the field of business, courses in mathematics, bookkeeping, accounts, currency and kindred subjects. Of late years the High School has been one of the chief centers of interest in the field of education. Its courses of studies have been greatly extended and its standards raised. The young men who enter Harvard by way of the High School have

SCHOOL AND COLLEGE

made an exceptionally high record in their entrance examinations.

There is a small group of endowed preparatory schools for boys; some of which, like the academies at Exeter and Andover, are of early origin; others, like St. Paul's, Lawrenceville, Groton, the Hill School, the Mercersberg Academy, are of later creation. These schools, which fill in the United States the place taken by Eton, Harrow, Rugby and other well-known public schools in England, are generously endowed, handsomely housed, and have behind them a growing body of graduates devoted to their interest.

Increasing numbers of American youth are prepared for college, however, in the High Schools. These schools have become, moreover, social centers in the smaller towns and in the larger and more widely scattered communities. They bring together boys and girls from country homes and rural hamlets, and no small part of the education they furnish is in the broadening of ideas and interests through this wider intercourse. There is a growing feeling that the fine, spacious and often beautiful buildings devoted to public education have larger uses for the community than they have yet served; night schools have long been established in the city school buildings and popular lectures on serious subjects are given in their assembly rooms. In some communities there is a growing disposition to place the school buildings more generally in the hands of the people for meetings called to discuss public questions or to take action on public matters.

At seventeen or eighteen the boy enters college and, if he takes the full college course, spends four years in further study of the languages, of mathematics, history, philosophy, science in its various departments, economics in its greatly broadened scope. Until a generation ago the course of study in the different colleges was practically identical so far as subjects were concerned; there were four classes, sometimes subdivided for the sake of efficiency, and each class followed a fixed course in the Humanities, in Philosophy, Mathematics and the principles of Science. The course was sharply defined

SCHOOL AND COLLEGE

and every student was compelled to conform to its requirements. There was then a perfectly defined and widely accepted conception of the college as an institution for the general education of youth on broad lines of liberal culture; an attempt to put into practice the definition of education formulated by Bishop Comenius: "to train generally all who are born men for all which is human."

The American college was the culmination of a course of education devised to train the boy as a general force before preparing him for specific uses of that force; to make him familiar with the history of thought, and with classical literature; to give him sound habits of thought and a general view of the physical world through a knowledge of the principles of Science. The word culture defined perhaps as accurately as a single word can define the older college ideal in America and described the quality which it developed in the best students. It was a literary rather than a scientific education, and reflected, with modifications, the English university ideals by which all the early colleges, except the University of Virginia, were deeply influenced. It sent out men of culture rather than men of thorough training; technical and professional education was provided by the universities and technical schools and followed at the end of the college course. Lowell, one of the finest examples of the generous culture of the old-time college, put the college ideal in somewhat exaggerated form in the declaration that a college should teach nothing useful; nothing, that is, which a man turns to account in earning a living. The college was supposed to help a man "make his soul" — to borrow a French phrase; the special training which came later taught him to make his living.

But radical changes of general conditions have greatly modified and extended the older college curriculum. The development of the sciences has compelled the introduction of departments, of subdivisions of classes, of extended laboratory facilities; and the spread of scientific ideas and the immensely widened uses of science have put scientific interests in the forefront of the

SCHOOL AND COLLEGE

higher education and, in a great number of institutions, revolutionized both the subjects and the methods of college training.

Formerly the majority of American youth looked forward to one of three professions, the law, medicine or theology. These were called the "learned professions," because it was recognized that special training was of high importance in their practice. Now there are more than a hundred professions which demand technical training on the part of their practitioners; and engineering, which only a few men formerly chose for their life work, now has not only its own schools in connection with the older universities but has called into existence a large number of institutions of high rank devoted entirely to its own educational work.

Formerly, before the relations between business and science had been recognized — and in this respect Japan and Germany are far in the lead — the youth who intended to enter into any form of commercial life learned his work by entering an established business house and working his way up from the bottom.

AMERICAN IDEALS

Not only was he not expected to bring a college training to his task, but such a training was regarded as a hindrance to his success; it brought him too late into the field and it gave him ideas, habits and tastes which were of no practical service. Men of business regarded the college as useful in preparing men for the professions, but as unnecessary if not a hindrance to success in dealing with practical affairs. But competition with countries in which business is as much a profession as the Law or Medicine or Diplomacy, and the steadily advancing standards of efficiency in all fields of endeavor, have compelled the reorganization of the methods of higher education. The heads of great manufacturing organizations have learned that a main source of profit lies in the skill of the chemist, and that the laboratories of the universities hold the success of the factories in their hands; and it has become difficult to keep promising young chemists in the field of original research because business offers such glittering prizes and such rapid advancement.

SCHOOL AND COLLEGE

The immense development of the means of transportation has opened another field of endeavor to trained men, and service in the various scientific departments of the government still another field. Farming is put on a scientific basis, and a large number of schools and colleges of agriculture have come into existence.

These new demands on education have been met in the college curriculum as well as in the development of universities and technical schools. The colleges which still hold to the older ideal of education as a discipline to secure culture have responded by enlarging and equipping their facilities for the study of science. But the great majority of colleges have gone much further: they have provided a very wide range of studies, and given their students, under certain restrictions, the privilege of electing which road they will take to obtain the degree which becomes more and more necessary to the man who hopes for preferment in any profession or occupation that demands the knowledge of the expert.

AMERICAN IDEALS

The elective system has now been tested by the experience of a generation; and while it has been modified so as to secure a certain logical order and a certain coördination of studies, it has permanently established itself in many colleges. Scientific and humanistic courses run parallel with one another through the four years and lead to degrees in science or in art as the case may be. This involves the subdivision of classes into small groups, the enlargement of faculties, the extension of equipment to include laboratories, departmental libraries, rooms for the seminar, for apparatus of many kinds; and all these things have added enormously to the expense of education.

It has been found necessary, moreover, to provide for those young men who cannot command the time and money necessary for both college and university training but to whom the degree in Law, Medicine, Engineering, Pedagogy, Theology is essential. If a man takes the full college course he graduates, as a rule, at twenty-two years of age and still has three or four years of work in the

SCHOOL AND COLLEGE

Medical, Law, Theological or Technical school before he can begin his work in life. In other words, he cannot begin to earn his own living until he is twenty-five or twenty-six years of age. It is true very large endowments in the hands of the colleges provide aid for an army of students who cannot meet all their expenses; and many colleges, especially those in cities, provide the student with facilities for earning money in ways which do not conflict with academic duties. But there are many students who cannot postpone self-support so late; and some colleges have responded to their needs by furnishing opportunities for professional and technical education during the last two years of the college course, counting the work done in these years in the sum total of required work for the coveted degree which opens the doors of the several professions. By this means the time of preparation is reduced one or two years. But there is a strong feeling in favor of the full course whenever conditions permit.

In a number of colleges the elective system

exists in the modified form of the group system; and students are offered, not a free choice of a wide range of unrelated studies, but of groups of studies so arranged as to cover various fields and to provide a fairly consistent and logical scheme of general education. Even in colleges which provide most generously for elective students it has been found necessary to place incoming students under the influence of experienced advisers in making their initial choice of subjects and to require certain definite attainments for a degree.

The student instinct for choosing easy, or, in the student slang, "snap," courses has also been put under police regulation, so to speak. In a word, the endeavor has been made to protect the undergraduate from his own inexperience in planning his college course, to secure from him at least a respectable amount of work, and to make sure that he gets a fairly comprehensive view of the field of knowledge.

Very broad contrasts are offered therefore by the American college; in many insti-

SCHOOL AND COLLEGE

tutions the students still pursue through four years the beaten paths in Latin, Greek, History, Philosophy, Literature, Natural Science and Mathematics; in other institutions, of which Harvard may serve as an example, the field of knowledge is traversed by paths so many as to bewilder the Freshman who is eager to make the best use of his opportunities. It is said that a man could not take all the courses offered at Harvard in two hundred years. Every student is required to study English composition; beyond this very modest requirement the whole field is practically open to him. The Harvard system, which has been somewhat modified, is the ultimate expression of New England individualism in education. It is reported that in a certain university of recent creation the President, a man of notable scholarship and unappeasable energy, was waited upon one morning by a young man who wished to study Choctaw, a vanishing Indian dialect. "We have no department for the teaching of Choctaw this morning," said the head of the university, "but if you will be good enough to call again this afternoon we will organize one for you."

There are no stories which bring us nearer to the American spirit than the stories of patient self-denial and self-sacrifice of parents in order that their children may be educated. To bring together the sum necessary for this purpose the father and mother will strip their lives of every comfort and pleasure.

Fifty years ago it was the boy who filled the foreground of hope and ambition; but for a generation the girl has stood beside him. She looks forward to a college course as confidently as her brother; and for her it has become as necessary if she is to enter the profession which has long been open to women in America, teaching. But the vast majority of girls who take the college course are not and do not expect to become self-supporting. They come from well-to-do homes; they are the children of professional men, of the leading officers of the government, of men of large means; as well as of teachers on small salaries, of farmers on small farms, and of village shopkeepers. The college woman has long ceased

SCHOOL AND COLLEGE

to be a marked person; she is taken for granted in every community; and she is foremost in all kinds of good work. Colleges for women have come into existence in all parts of the country; many of them well endowed, amply and often nobly housed, and offering courses which parallel the courses in the colleges for men and lead to the same degrees upon almost identical conditions. Vassar College, founded in 1865, led the way in providing for the higher education of women and remains in the forefront; but Smith, Bryn Mawr, Mt. Holyoke, Radcliffe, Wells, Wellesley and other institutions of high rank have come into being in response to an ever-widening demand; and to-day one of the most serious problems which colleges for women face is the overtaxing of their facilities for housing and teaching an army of eager girls.

While college education for women was in the experimental stage, the courses closely paralleled those in colleges for men; but college training for women has demonstrated its usefulness and is as much a part of the American system as college training for men, and a distinct differentiation of educational material and method is taking place; the colleges for women giving increasing attention to science as applied to the home, to sanitation, to the chemistry of foods and to household economics. That line of cleavage will become more apparent as time goes on, and the college will apply science to home making and home keeping as it applies science to the various occupations in which men are engaged.

The influence of the English university on the American college is seen in the great importance attached to physical well-being in the various forms of sport. Americans were slow to follow the mother country in its devotion to sport, but during the last quarter of a century they have developed a love of athletics which has created a different atmosphere, not only in the colleges but in the country. It is often said in Europe that Americans are absorbed in business; but no one can read the long, detailed and technical reports of sports by land and water, which are as much a feature of the daily newspaper

SCHOOL AND COLLEGE

in America as cable dispatches from Tokyo, Paris, Berlin or London, without recognizing the keen and well-nigh universal interest in these matters. Nor can any one see the crowds that hang breathless on the issue of games of baseball and football, or hear the thunder of the cheers that roll in great waves across hotly combatted college fields, without sharing the eagerness of spirit with which Americans play as well as work. Save in pioneering and agricultural districts, Americans were once an indoors people; they are now an out-of-doors people, proficient not only in sport of all kinds but finding keen delight in the life of the woods and in the open air.

For many years the growing interest in athletics among students was looked upon with apprehension by men bred in the older college traditions, and there has been some ground for that apprehension. Too much time has been devoted to athletics, the perspective of values has been distorted, and the heroes of the undergraduate world have been not the winners of the prizes in intellectual contests but the champion kicker and quarterback, the pitcher and batter who play baseball with the precision of the great billiard experts. The intercollegiate contests have brought in a keen competitive spirit and laid too great a burden of business management on undergraduates. At the annual football contest between Yale and Harvard forty thousand people are often present, the money received for admissions at the gates exceeds seventy-five thousand dollars. The university has a stadium which seats thirty-eight thousand spectators.

The evils of excessive devotion to athletics are being remedied; its benefits are many and great. The games are fundamentally educational; many who visit Oxford and Cambridge in the spring and early summer and find the student body on the fields and the river do not realize that these sports, pursued in the amateur spirit, are as valuable a feature of university training as the work done in the lecture rooms and the laboratory. They make men of great physical vigor and endurance, of vigorous will and ability to

SCHOOL AND COLLEGE

gain or lose with equal steadiness. Much of the organizing power and the unyielding courage which have made the English name respected at the ends of the earth were developed on the fields of the Public Schools and of the Universities which have trained the leaders of the state at home and abroad.

Physical training of scientific thoroughness is a feature of the American college and has a place in the educational system almost as important as that which the Greeks gave it. Lacking the artistic sense which made Greek athletics sculpturesque, American athletics have raised the moral standards of the undergraduate community by supplying legitimate channels for the overflowing energies of youth, by teaching the laws of health, and by defining manly ideals of life. In Yale University, which has long been a leader in college athletics, there is a phrase which expresses what is called the Yale spirit: "fair play and team play." This phrase means that in all contests the game shall be played according to the rules and that the players shall so subordinate themselves that the team shall play as one man. No country has been more fortunate than Japan in the training of a thousand years in "team play," nor has any ever given a more striking demonstration of its effectiveness. The members of the baseball and football teams in American colleges submit to rules of living far more rigid than those which govern the army, and to a discipline in subordination and obedience not less exacting. The games have become largely contests of skill; they are won by strategy, by signals for which every man waits, and by the devotion which capitalizes the total strength and skill of a group of men and directs them as a commander directs his troops when the battle is on.

The vital interest which students take in athletics is one of the various forms through which the college community expresses itself; for in the American college the curriculum and the scheme of training are parts of that larger whole which is called college life, and which defines the whole range of student interests and activities: the social intercourse, which is generally of a most wholesome and

SCHOOL AND COLLEGE

manly kind, the generous opportunity for fellowship and friendship, the literary associations, the free discussion of all open questions, — and to-day there are no closed questions, — the scientific societies which bring together small groups of men of kindred tastes, the publication of newspapers and magazines, and the dramatic organizations; these activities supplement and sometimes supplant the regular work which the undergraduate is supposed to do. The card on the wall of a student's room which read "in this room study if not allowed to interfere with the regular course of college life" was not wholly humorous; for athletic, literary, journalistic and social interests are so many that the popular student has little time for serious study.

In the older colleges there is a good deal of picturesque idleness; there is very little vice, but much wasting of time. A majority of students, however, pursue their work with fidelity if not with enthusiasm, and get a kind of atmospheric education which makes them more agreeable companions and more

AMERICAN IDEALS

interesting men. For college life is regulated by generous ideals of honor, of friendship, and of loyalty, which have a more penetrating influence than most teachers are able to command; and the sentiment which inspires college songs, and which stirs the heart of the graduate long years afterwards, is an expression of the generous idealism which is or ought to be the unfailing offering of youth to the well-being of the race.

The American college is a product of American conditions and holds a large place in the interest and affection of the people. It perpetuates the tradition of liberal learning which had its modern birth in the University of Paris in the Middle Ages, which has given to Oxford and Cambridge a quality that has enriched the literature and the life of the English people; and which, carried across the sea, has been shared by a great Democracy without loss of its largeness of vision and its power of liberating men from the narrowness of local interests and provincial prejudices.

IX

UNIVERSITY AND RESEARCH WORK

The college in America preceded the university because it was needed earlier in the development of the country; and, with loyalty to certain deep-seated traditions which came with the colonists, it has adapted itself to American conditions. In no other country are the higher institutions of learning more intimately related to the life of the people. This is seen in the large space given to college affairs in the daily newspapers, and in the position of the heads of colleges and universities in public regard.

The educational leaders are public men as truly as the governors of States or the members of the President's Cabinet. They are almost invariably represented on all commissions appointed by the government to study industrial, social or political conditions; they are called upon to interpret public events on notable occasions; they are often appointed to fill the most distinguished positions in the gift of the government. When President Lincoln made the address at Gettysburg, which is one of the classics of American oratory and the noblest definition of American political ideals, the formal oration was delivered by an ex-President of Harvard University, who had also been American Ambassador, or Minister, in London; John Quincy Adams, the fifth President of the United States, held a professorship in the same institution. Lowell, who at a later time taught literature in Harvard, was one of the most influential diplomatists ever sent by the United States to London. The head of the University of Michigan represented his country at Constantinople during the Spanish-American War. The President of Cornell University is now American Minister in Athens. The retirement of Dr. Eliot from the presidency of Harvard was made the subject of extended editorial comment by the newspapers from Boston to San Francisco; and Signor Ferraro, the Italian historian who was then in the United States, declared that

UNIVERSITY AND RESEARCH WORK

in no other country would the retirement of the head of a university awaken such widespread public interest. And it is an open secret that the position of Ambassador to Great Britain was offered to Dr. Eliot and declined.

Although higher education in America is not under governmental control, the needs of the country have largely determined its scope and direction, and the university has been as definitely the creation of American conditions as the college. It was the product of a later age. The personality of teachers does not count for so much as in the college; it is further removed from the life of the country in the sense that the average citizen does not feel so much at home with it as with the college to which, often with great self-sacrifice, he has sent his children.

In the Central and Far West, however, he has had a great deal more to do with the shaping of the university and the direction of its activities than with the making of the college. The college was inherited; it was brought over the sea with the religious convictions and social habits of his ancestors; the university, as he knows it, was born in his own state and has grown up with the society in which he lives.

In many parts of America the granting of degrees is within the power of those institutions only which conform to certain educational standards, but in other parts of the country the words college and university are sometimes assumed by institutions of a high school grade. In this field, as in others, the foreign observer must know local conditions so to speak. An authority on such matters has expressed the opinion that of the several hundred so-called colleges in the United States there are a hundred and twenty-five, perhaps one third of the number, which are effective, high-class institutions. The other so-called colleges often serve a useful purpose. They are open doors to a large number of boys and girls in remote localities, who would otherwise get only a common school education. They often grow into colleges; their fault is their misleading assumption of a rank to which they are not entitled.

UNIVERSITY AND RESEARCH WORK

Of endowed universities there are perhaps fifteen or twenty; and they are all of comparatively recent date. Some of them have developed from long-established colleges; more have been founded and built up within the last four or five decades. One of the most influential, the Johns Hopkins, recently celebrated its twenty-fifth anniversary, and the University of Chicago, one of the most amply equipped and vigorous of these younger institutions, has not yet reached its quarter of a century.

Among the first group, Harvard, Yale, Columbia, have grown by a normal process of evolution out of the old American college. They have gradually enlarged the scope of studies to meet the needs of a new economic age and have changed their organization and administration to cope with vastly increased numbers of teachers and students, not only by widening the field of study but by the development of more adequate methods of administration. Columbia University, in the city of New York, enrolls about six thousand students, and has an endowment of about

$40,000,000. Thirty years ago it had an attendance of three or four hundred. It has grown with the country and is in itself a history of American educational progress. Beginning in the early days of the colonies as a high school, it took on later the form and functions of a college because colleges were demanded by students who wished more advanced methods and studies. As the need for special training for the professions became more general, the college gradually transformed itself into a university.

A few of these institutions, like the Johns Hopkins University, the University of Chicago and the Leland Stanford University in California, were established by large endowments from private persons. The gifts of the founder of the University of Chicago to that institution exceed forty millions of dollars. In several instances a university has been completely organized in advance; a group of buildings planned, a large group of teachers secured, and libraries and laboratories equipped for work. The rapid construction of buildings of recent years, in which im-

UNIVERSITY AND RESEARCH WORK

proved machinery and continuous labor secure speedy results without loss of solidity or thoroughness, has been paralleled in the establishment of colleges and universities. Such institutions lack the traditions and associations with eminent persons which give the older schools an atmosphere that appeals to the imagination and defines the standards of achievement; but they often become from the start highly effective, not only in imparting knowledge but in the field of research. Within a decade of its foundation the publications of the Johns Hopkins University found place in the reading rooms of European universities and were read by scholars in all parts of the world. The first President of this university adopted a policy, not always pursued in America, of using large means, not to erect great buildings but to bring together distinguished scholars in the teaching body.

A third and larger group of universities has come into existence to meet the demand for free education by the States. From modest beginnings these institutions have grown into thoroughly equipped schools, numbering their attendance by thousands, and commanding great incomes yielded by a small percentage of the total tax laid by the State upon its citizens. The practical use of these institutions in the development of the agricultural, mining and manufacturing interests of the State have been so obvious that the taxpayers not only support but enforce a policy of generous appropriations for their support in the legislatures; and the remote small farmer feels that the university stands ready, not only to educate his children but to help him develop his farm. The head of one of these institutions said not long ago that his difficulty lay not in getting money but in wisely expending it. In the previous years his university has received from the State a sum of money equivalent to the income of an endowment of forty million dollars. From feeble beginnings in Georgia, Tennessee and North Carolina at the end of the eighteenth century State institutions doing thorough work are to be found; while in all the Western and in many other Southern States the state universities are housed in buildings of great

UNIVERSITY AND RESEARCH WORK

size, though not always of impressive architecture, and probably include in their membership three fourths of the three hundred and fifty thousand students in the American colleges and universities.

In the majority of these state institutions the courses of study are practical and vocational, though other studies are pursued; and the alertness and intellectual activity of the typical western college student keep him in touch with all the interests of the day. In the West all these institutions are largely attended by women.

The word university is applied in America to institutions of widely different types and standards. It may mean a State university which offers a great variety of practical studies and directs its research work chiefly if not wholly to applied science, in its relations to agriculture and industry. It may mean, and for many years it did mean, a college which has affiliated with itself schools of medicine, law and theology. Yale represents this type. It may mean an institution in which opportunities for advanced work are afforded, as in Harvard and the Johns Hopkins. It may mean an institution which provides courses of study in all departments of applied science. Lehigh is a typical institution of this kind. Or it may mean an institution devoted exclusively to laboratory methods and research work, for graduate students. Clark University is a leader in this field.

Of universities in the European sense there are perhaps fifteen or twenty in the United States, and these are organized largely on the lines of the German Universities. The first direct educational influence from Europe which made itself felt in America was English. Eighty-five years ago the first group of American students went to the German Universities after completing the college course at home. Their number gradually increased, for American youth were eager to carry their studies further than the American colleges made possible. By the middle of the last century men trained under German methods were represented on the faculties of the most progressive colleges, and under German influence these institutions were gradually modi-

UNIVERSITY AND RESEARCH WORK

fied to conform more closely to the German model. The English type gave place in considerable measure to the German type; and, while the English Grammar School stood as a model for the early classical school in the colonies, and Oxford and Cambridge furnished the ideals of the American college, the German Universities have greatly influenced the organization, methods and aims of American universities. For many years there was an increasing attendance of Americans in Berlin, Heidelberg and other German institutions, and the opportunities for advanced work at home were so limited that the student who looked forward to an academic career was practically compelled to supplement his study at home by study in some foreign university; to have studied abroad was not formally required of the men who sought places as teachers in the American colleges; but it was so generally expected that the man who lacked it was seriously handicapped.

This German influence, largely scientific in its direction, was reënforced by the increasing demand for men of scientific training in many important industries. It led to the introduction of the elective system, to the breaking up of the classes into divisions, to the widening of the field of study; and to a readjustment of educational values. It shifted the emphasis from the Humanities to the sciences, and put discipline and training on a level with culture as the chief ends of education.

German methods have not been slavishly followed, however, and the German influence is neither so direct nor so obvious as it was twenty years ago. Americans have adopted what was valuable for American uses in German methods as they had earlier adopted what was valuable in English methods, and have worked out their own educational scheme. To the English universities that scheme is greatly indebted for the classical tradition with its emphasis on quality and richness of the intellectual life, and to the German universities for a greatly enlarged range of study, for more thorough and scientific methods of work, for a strong impetus toward original investigation, and for high standards of technical training. The German influence has

UNIVERSITY AND RESEARCH WORK

involved some loss of interest in classical and literary studies and has blunted somewhat the sense of form and the feeling for the finer qualities of literary expression; it substituted literary scholarship for love of literature and for a time made the study of English largely a matter of philology. But the pendulum is swinging back, and in the teaching of English the literary spirit is making itself felt with an increasing effectiveness. In this field the French influence has come to the aid of the earlier ideals of literary study.

Opportunities for advanced work in the American Universities are now so ample that study in foreign universities, while not without its advantages, is no longer a necessity, and the number of Americans in German universities has greatly fallen off.

The need of highly trained men in many kinds of business, in enterprises requiring engineering skill of a high order, in mining, agriculture and the construction and management of railroads, has called into existence a large number of high-grade institutions of a scientific character, among the most promi-

AMERICAN IDEALS

nent of which are the Boston Institute of Technology, the Stevens Institute, the Troy Polytechnic, the Columbia School of Mines, and Lehigh University. These and other kindred institutions are scientific universities.

In no department have the standards of preparation been more rapidly advanced than in teaching. Pedagogy is comparatively a new science in America, but it has taken a place of the first importance in public regard. In the higher grades of school work, college and normal school degrees or certificates are now required. The State universities have made ample provision for pedagogic training, normal schools are part of the public school system in every state; and in the Teachers College, affiliated with Columbia University in New York, advanced courses in educational work are provided and are attended by large numbers of students whose enthusiasm is the best evidence of the vitality of its methods. In Clark University, an institution for research which is doing a notable work in training teachers for colleges and universities, this department is specially well equipped, and its

UNIVERSITY AND RESEARCH WORK

President, Dr. G. Stanley Hall, has been one of the prophets of pedagogy in America.

There is a marked tendency to bring technical training of all kinds into close relation with the universities. Many medical, law and theological schools, and schools of applied science, were originally established on an independent basis and the entrance requirements made it possible for men to specialize on a very inadequate foundation of general knowledge. The medical student came to his professional studies without even a high school diploma; he often went straight from the farm to the lecture room and the clinic; and this was also true in a measure of the theological and law student. This lack of coordination no longer exists; many professional schools are open only to students who have completed a college course or its equivalent; and those schools which have grown up as independent institutions have affiliated themselves with universities and, without losing their individuality, have come into relations with other departments of knowledge and have conformed to more scientific methods of teaching.

AMERICAN IDEALS

Meantime, as has been said, the colleges have modified their courses so as to offer the student opportunities of taking some of his professional work as part of his college work and in this way shortening the time to his ultimate graduation. This tendency will undoubtedly lead in the end to the complete coöperation of the professional school and the university and to the taking over by the university of all forms of advanced training. This will mean not only greater economy and efficiency of management, but broader opportunities for the professional student, the freer atmosphere of university life and a better perspective of life in general.

The universities fill a great place in America and are steadily increasing their influence. They guard the gates of the professions and challenge the applicant for admission to prove his fitness to discharge the duties that fall to him. They have largely created the demand for thorough preparation for the pursuit of callings, which, like the practice of law and of medicine, are essentially public functions and require public regulation.

UNIVERSITY AND RESEARCH WORK

They teach the army of teachers whose function is also a public function. They train the chemists, engineers and men of affairs upon whose integrity and skill the nation depends for safety and prosperity. Their influence has contributed to the movement which is taking the administrative side of the government out of politics and placing it on a basis of merit and permanency of tenure. To them is committed the work of advancing knowledge by investigation and research; not only by "seeking knowledge wherever it may be found," to recall a noble phrase of the late Emperor of Japan, but to add to that capital of knowledge which is the common possession of all nations. They have already removed the reproach that American scholarship, while highly effective in transmitting knowledge, has made no notable contributions to its sum total. The work of education in a new country was immediate and engrossing, but the time has now come when the universities are able to take their place with institutions in the Old World in advancing the skirmish line of knowledge.

AMERICAN IDEALS

A group of great foundations have been created during the past few years, which aim not only to provide for and promote research, but to reënforce the specific endowments for higher education. The Carnegie Institution of Washington administers a fund of about $42,000,000, which may be regarded as the capitalization of research. The directors of this fund are given large discretion in the selection of objects, persons or enterprises to be aided; the general purpose being to give support to forms of research which require prolonged effort, to provide opportunities for original work by men of notable ability and efficiency, and to make possible the publication of the results of these ventures in the field of knowledge. The income of this fund may be devoted to scientific, geographical, or purely scholarly investigation, and may be expended in a variety of enterprises or concentrated in some field in which the need or the immediate promise of greater knowledge is pressing.

The Rockefeller Institute for Medical Research in the city of New York is an experi-

UNIVERSITY AND RESEARCH WORK

ment station for the investigation of diseases and of possible prevention and remedies. It has already rendered signal service to the country by putting expert service in coöperation with the medical profession, by stimulating the scientific spirit in that profession, and by concentrating investigation on pressing medical problems.

The widest field of work is that occupied by the General Education Board, which administers various large funds. The activities of this board are directed to three main purposes: the improvement of agriculture in the Southern States, the development of high schools in that section, and the promotion of higher education in all parts of the country. This fund amounts to nearly $33,000,000, and the net income is about $1,700,000. Last year forty-two colleges were aided by gifts amounting to $1,300,000. Large sums were devoted to demonstration work for farmers and for the reënforcement of schools in the south.

A fund which constitutes a great endowment for the colleges and universities in the

AMERICAN IDEALS

country which meet certain tests of educational efficiency is administered by the Carnegie Foundation for the Advancement of Teaching, which distributes annually the income of $15,000,000 in retiring allowances for college and university teachers who have reached the age of sixty-five years and have been in service for twenty-five years. In 1910 the number of beneficiaries of this fund was 364, and the average allowance paid was nearly $1,900,000. This provision for the old age of teachers has contributed greatly to the stability and attractiveness of academic teaching; and, reënforced by the pension systems of individual colleges, has relieved a host of able and devoted men rendering the highest service to the nation on salaries too small to make provision for old age possible, of the pressure of anxiety for the future support of their families. In many colleges provision is made for a year's leave of absence on half-salary every seven years.

Large funds are also expended by the Southern Education Board, which has greatly stimulated educational progress in the South-

UNIVERSITY AND RESEARCH WORK

ern States, and deals with educational conditions in that part of the country from a strategic point of view; concentrating its help at points where the need of immediate assistance is most pressing.

The Russell Sage Foundation, organized five years ago with an endowment of $10,000,000, has for its object the investigation and eradication, so far as is possible, of "The Causes of Poverty and Ignorance," and its work is already beginning to show fruit. It serves among other purposes as a center of information concerning the work of hundreds of social settlements, improvement clubs and organizations for social betterment maintained by women's clubs, college societies and private organizations in cities in all parts of the country. This fund not only conducts investigations but affords practical relief.

In a broader field a work of high educational importance is conducted by the Carnegie Endowment for International Peace, which expends yearly the income of a fund of $10,000,000, in the maintenance of a division of international law which is collecting all the data bearing on international arbitration; a Division of Economics and History, which is making a scientific study of the historical and economic causes of war; and a Division of Intercourse and Education.

These funds constitute a great endowment for advanced and aggressive educational work in the United States, and show the widespread interest in education among Americans, and their faith in its efficiency in the development of the national resources and life. During the last decade the gifts from private donors for education have aggregated at least $100,000,000.

X

THE AMERICAN AND HIS GOVERNMENT

THE stages of growth through which Japan, India, China, England and the nations of Europe passed in the legendary age the United States passed through under the eyes, so to speak, of the scientific historian. Mystery envelops the origins of other great peoples, and when they emerge into clear light they are racially unified and think, feel and act as nations. They are jealous of foreign influence; they regard the stranger with suspicion and treat him with disfavor. This is the early history of every people, Asiatic or European. The line of race descent is guarded with the utmost care and its purity becomes a matter of national concern. As a matter of fact, however, there is no absolute purity of race; and there ought to be none if variety and richness of temperament, intellectual

AMERICAN IDEALS

and moral trait, capacity for creative and practical activity, are essential to the complete expression of the human spirit. It is as easy to trace the Danish, Saxon and Norman strains in English art and history as to trace the hand of these vanished races in wall and road, in castle and church; and English life and character have been immensely energized and enriched by this commingling of races. To-day, however, we do not remember the Dane, the Saxon, the Norman when we speak of England; we think of a people who stand out distinctly from the peoples which surround them. In England, as in Japan, the fusion was accomplished so long ago that its stages have passed out of sight and the world sees only a completely developed nation.

In the United States this process of growth has taken place not behind closed doors as is the case of other nations, but in full view of the world; and the idea held by some writers that the Americans are a conglomeration of races without unity of ideal, national feeling or tradition, is as misleading as the idea that England is a mere aggregation of peoples of different blood. All nations are composite. The intermingling of races in America is only later in point of time; and, as a result of the American system, the assimilation of the national spirit is extraordinarily rapid. The atmosphere has a transforming quality. There is nothing more moving in the United States than the spectacle of two thousand Jewish children, whose parents have not yet learned to speak the English language, rising in their places in the assembly rooms of one of the city schools to salute the flag, or the ardor with which a group of recently arrived Italian immigrants will sing the national anthem.

It must not be forgotten that the earlier settlers in the New World, though of different races, were of a kindred spirit. The families from which they came were not far apart in point of development; they were of kindred rather than alien races; above all, they were moved by a few powerful motives which sent them on a common adventure, and developed in them qualities which prepared them for united action. They differed widely in religious convictions, in political ideals and in social habits; but they were all seekers after a larger freedom of action, more ample opportunities of personal and family life. To secure these things they braved great dangers and endured great hardships; for the most part they were adventurers of the nobler sort; seekers after the better fortunes of the race: freedom to think their own thoughts and live their own lives, better conditions for their children, more room for activity.

Shut off from Europe by the peril and length of the voyage across the ocean; encircled by vigilant foes; sharing the fortunes of pioneers on a remote frontier, the colonists were driven together by the conditions in which they lived and by a colonial policy which bore heavily upon them all and bred a growing discontent in every colony. The English, the Scotch, the Dutch brought with them well-defined ideas of political liberty; while the French, driven from their old homes by the tyranny of an arbitrary personal government, found the air of the New World stimulating to the impulse toward freedom.

AMERICAN AND HIS GOVERNMENT

When the long-smoldering antagonism against Great Britain became actual rebellion, the colonies stood together in a common cause. Their unity was marred by petty social jealousies, but they rapidly learned coöperation, and when the hour for the adoption of the Constitution arrived there was an American people to accept it as the formal organization of a nation. Magna Charta, the Bill of Rights, the Act of Settlement, registered the will of the English people; the Constitution proclaimed in Japan in 1893 is an impressive revelation of the hidden forces, the secret sources of strength in the Japanese character; but neither the English nor the Japanese nation was created by these memorable documents. The fourth day of July, on which the Declaration of Independence was signed in 1776, is celebrated as the birthday of the United States, but on that day the Americans were already a people in the same sense in which the English and Japanese are peoples. They were not made a nation by written documents; they dictated the documents. The language of the Declaration of Independence

AMERICAN IDEALS

is significant; it is not a definition of the purpose of the colonists to become independent; it begins with the statement "That these United Colonies *are*, and of right ought to be, free and independent states." In other words there was already in 1776 an American people, who held a common view of their status and rights and were ready to act together to maintain them. The different races were already, a century and a quarter after the first feeble attempt to build a home on the edge of the continent, welded together by common ideals of political order and fused into one people by their experiences in the New World.

They were the children of a century in which the human spirit had a new birth in energy of imagination, in faith in its power to dare greatly and achieve greatly. Shakespeare in the world of creative art; Drake and Frobisher in the world of adventure and action; Milton the singer, and Cromwell the soldier, half a century later, were the leaders of a movement of expansion which not only created a greater England over seas, but gave the English spirit the freedom of a greater world. The Puritan in New England; the exiled cavalier in Virginia; the persecuted Friends in Pennsylvania; the Huguenots in New York and South Carolina, to whom their convictions were dearer than the fair fields of France; the hardy Scotch-Irish; had all felt the powerful influence which had turned the eyes of adventurous men in many countries to the New World, and daring spirits everywhere had responded to the cry heard on the Thames in Shakespeare's time: "Westward Ho!" There were among the colonists men who hated the rigid formalities of life in the Old World; men for whom the free life of the frontier had an irresistible attraction; and there were also a small group who found in the wilderness a refuge from courts and jails.

To these builders of communities along the Atlantic coast the spirit of the eighteenth century, the age both of reason and of sentiment, of Hume and Locke, of Voltaire and Rousseau, of the daring speculators who made ready for the Revolution in France, gave not only a fresh impulse toward freedom of thought, but a philosophical basis for the

AMERICAN IDEALS

democratic order. In 1776 the colonists were still a feeble folk, but they had gained self-confidence; they had been alienated from Europe by a policy which was as stupid as it was arbitrary; and they were becoming conscious of the possession of a vast estate. A few among their leaders already had visions of the nation that was to be long after the independence had been achieved. These and other influences had combined to make an American people and to make an American spirit. It is easier to describe a spirit than to define it; and a description is mainly an enumeration of qualities. In such an analysis skill lies as much in what is omitted as in what is included; for, while many qualities give the spirit of a people shading and proportion, a few qualities give it the distinction of aim and emotional content which make it possible to differentiate the Japanese, the French, the English and the American spirit.

The most obvious expression of the American spirit is the political organization of the nation. Local governments manage local affairs, build and maintain schools, make

AMERICAN AND HIS GOVERNMENT

roads, enforce sanitary conditions, impose and collect taxes; county governments regulate the affairs of larger units of political organizations; State governments direct the affairs of the forty-eight States into which the country is divided, as Japan is divided into provinces; and a National government, composed of the President, the executive head of the government; the Congress, consisting of a House of Representatives elected directly by the people; and a smaller body, the Senate, elected by the legislatures of the States, manage the affairs of the nations. The Supreme Court, a group of nine judges appointed by the President for life unless removed by the very rare process of impeachment, has power to declare acts of Congress unconstitutional, and as the official interpreter of the Constitution, so to speak, has had a great part in shaping the political development of the country.

The Constitution not only created the form of government under which the American people have lived since 1789 and defined its functions, but definitely limited the authority of that government and guaranteed the rights

AMERICAN IDEALS

of the individual citizen, not only as against the invasion of other citizens but against their invasion by the government or itself. The American Bill of Rights is incorporated in the Constitution. Foreign students of the American system have found it difficult to understand because, as a distinguished English publicist has said, they have been unable to discover where the supreme power, the sovereignty, is placed. That sovereignty cannot be found in the government; it does not inhere in the President, in the Supreme Court or in Congress; nor does it lodge in the forty-eight States which now compose the United States. The sovereignty is neither in the Constitution nor in the government organized under it; it is in the people of the United States, who made the Constitution and reserved to themselves the sole right to change it by addition or amendment; a right which they have already exercised sixteen times. It follows almost as a matter of course that the Constitution is a definition of principles, not a code of laws or a body of regulations.

Under this flexible system American life

AMERICAN AND HIS GOVERNMENT

has developed with such freedom that the hand of the Federal government has hardly been felt by the private citizen. The system of indirect taxation has left his pocket untouched, and the government at Washington has been something about which he has talked much, but for which, except in great crises, he has done little; not through lack of patriotism but because its demands upon him have been so few. This freedom from burdens has made possible some of the problems with which Americans are dealing to-day; entire absence of oversight and control of great business enterprises has made room for serious abuses of privilege, for the creation of private monopolies, for oppressive discrimination against individuals and communities, for indifference to the interests both of the public and of investors. An unexampled prosperity has so completely absorbed the activities of the country that the inadequacy of law to meet the new conditions was not recognized until gross abuses began to stir public indignation and call for governmental action.

The War between the States compelled

the Federal government, as a matter of self-preservation, to assume powers not before exercised, and new conditions have compelled it to assume closer relations with the life of the people; but it has never been the supreme expression of that life. The sovereign might have said at any moment *"l'état, c'est moi,"* for the sovereign is the people. The American has conceived of his government as existing to keep the house in order while the family lived its life freely, every individual following the bent of his own genius within well-defined limits of social law. Political and public life have never been synonymous. There has been no lack of able men in the service of the government, but the government has been one of a number of channels through which the life of the nation has flowed. That life has been of far greater volume than the political history of the nation accounts for.

Into the field of individual action the American government does not enter; in that field, in which lie religion, the family education, science, professional activity, finance, commerce, business, journalism, there

AMERICAN AND HIS GOVERNMENT

has been entire freedom for individual energy and ability. Public opinion controls the government, and the leaders of this opinion have been as often at the bar, in the universities, in the pulpit, in the editor's chair, as in the White House or in Congress.

The National government found itself the owner of immense tracts of unoccupied land, and for many years this land was practically given away to all who were willing to develop it; and there are now three thousand miles of farms from the Atlantic to the Pacific, extending over an area between Canada and Mexico a thousand miles wide. There are, therefore, an unprecedented number of private owners of property in the country; of men who have an interest in social and political stability and who will act as a conservative force in any economic or social crisis through which the nation may pass. The national territory has been so vast that until within the last two decades there has always been a frontier.

It has taken the Americans nearly three centuries to get their estate under cultivation, and during the whole period of their existence as a people, they have exhibited contemporaneously all stages of social development, from the most stable and conservative to the most changeable and radical; from cities which mark the location of the earliest colonies, Boston and New York, Washington and Charleston, to the mining camp and the cattle range. This is one of the facts about America which foreigners find it difficult to understand, and when they read of the robbery of a stagecoach in a lonely defile of the Sierra Nevadas, they forget that they are reading of a section still in the frontier stage of development and not far removed from the time when isolated communities were compelled to make and execute their own laws. The new communities formed by the continuous stream of settlers who have moved westward have passed through all the stages of political organization which have been characteristic of the American system. In the earliest and rudest conditions they have governed themselves; the instinct for order in the American, developed by many centuries of steadily widening self-government, is so much a part of him that

AMERICAN AND HIS GOVERNMENT

in the most remote mining camp, among men of the roughest habits, some kind of local order is established. As the communities have grown, they have been organized into territories, which is the final stage before statehood; and as soon as the population has met the requirements, the territory has been admitted as a state.

The whole process, however, has been carried on by individual initiative; and not until a sufficient number of individuals have united have the privileges of State or National government been accorded to them.

Under a political system so flexible and free, on a territory of vast extent awaiting settlement, a people with the political antecedents and the disciplinary experience of the Americans have exhibited certain traits which may be regarded as national characteristics, creating what may be called the American spirit.

The American has learned to take care of himself; he does not expect the government to take care of him. Many of the services which are rendered to the individual in other countries he performs for himself. He has so long taken the possession of individual freedom for granted, that he expects the government to do as little as possible for him or with him. He asks for a free field and a fair chance; the rest he expects to do for himself. He chooses his own form of religion, his school, his college, his profession, his wife, his place of residence, his manner of life, his recreations. He objects to any supervision of these personal affairs, and he is accepting government regulation of certain forms of business, not because he likes it, but because he sees that it is necessary. When he travels abroad he recognizes and enjoys the help which governments more paternal in character render to their citizens; but long habit has accustomed him to rely on himself at home.

He is jealous of his personal independence and he is self-reliant. These qualities brought his ancestors to the New World, created the political conditions under which he lives, and have developed the country. He expects to support his church, to contribute to the charities of his neighborhood or town, to help endow schools, colleges and hospitals. If he pays taxes to support a State University he expects that university to work with and for the state. He gives more and more generously to build and endow art museums and hospitals, to create parks, to secure from business uses national scenery. The largeness of modern undertakings and their interstate relations are accustoming him to the appearance of the government in new fields and exercising larger powers; but if a monument is to be built, a college endowed in some neglected section, a reform movement set on foot, his first thought is to call together a few influential men and give individual initiative the force and influence of public not governmental organization. The first impulse comes from the individual, and individual initiative has been perhaps the prime element in the development of the country. Such educational institutions as Hampton Institute, Tuskegee, and Berea College, doing work of the highest importance, were created by individuals.

To the general statement of the reliance of the individual on his own exertions without aid from the government there has been one notable and profoundly influential exception. The policy of protection has hastened and developed American industries and has added immensely to the wealth of the country. But, aside from its commercial value, it has had one very disastrous effect: it has accustomed a very large class of business interests to look to the government for aid in the building up of private enterprises. The government has become, in effect, the silent partner in many manufacturing industries, and great business interests have become so involved with political action that a system of trading grew up between a certain class of politicians and certain protected industries, which has been the source of widespread political corruption. This state of things has set in motion a determined and successful effort to make an end of an unnatural alliance. The tariff of the future will be out of politics. Even when they have sought the aid of the government, some Americans have regarded the national authority as their servant and have used it to advance their private fortunes.

AMERICAN AND HIS GOVERNMENT

Emerson, who is the prophet as well as the poet of the American political and social order, defined America in one significant word: opportunity. It has not only held its entrance doors open to all comers, but it has kept the inner doors open, so that a man might pass from room to room as fast and as long as he had the strength to open the doors. Education, fortune and station have been and are open to all; the penniless boy has become the head of a leading university, the governor of his state or its senator; the frontier young man, without opportunity of formal education but with the passion for knowledge and impelled by a noble ambition, has become President. In America the goals are many and the race is open to all; success is largely a question of ability and endurance.

There are no fixed and permanent social and economic classes in the country and there is a settled determination that there never shall be; that the field shall be kept open and that all shall strive under impartial conditions, with special privileges to none. The doctrine of political equality does not mean social,

AMERICAN IDEALS

intellectual or economic equality: it means equality of opportunity to all men to put forth their energy and to win and keep the rewards of their ability, character and industry.

The American boy grows up in a stimulating atmosphere. He is familiar from his earliest youth with the romances of heroic endeavor. The story of honorable success is told in a thousand forms, but its elements are few and obvious; character, self-reliance, courage, industry. During the last thirty years the opportunities of fortune making have been unprecedented and have presented unprecedented temptations to unfair and tyrannical dealing, and many men have fallen victims to the desire to make great fortunes over night, so to speak; but many instances of prosperous dishonor — if dishonor can ever be prosperous — have not blurred the essential soundness and integrity of American success.

The New World was settled by men who expected to better their conditions and that expectation has been and is a constant force in American life. The boy expects to be a

AMERICAN AND HIS GOVERNMENT

man of influence and fortune; the local banker expects to become a financier; the small trader expects to become a great merchant; the obscure young scholar dreams of the opportunities of a chair in the university; the rising lawyer, with an instinct for public affairs, anticipates the honor of political station and leadership. Every man in America is looking forward; the country is always planning for the future. That future is not, however, a vague hope, a mere expectation; it is an enormous national asset because it stands for a volume of undeveloped resources which are tangible and, in large measure, calculable; the development of which is a matter of time and capital. This sense of futurity is inevitable in a country which is still largely undeveloped. There has been a little intoxication in the air and it has sometimes found its way into the popular speech. But the "tall talk" which Dickens found both offensive and amusing is heard to-day only in hotly contested elections or in the mouths of the representatives of remote rural constituencies. The average American is amused or bored by it.

AMERICAN IDEALS

An Englishman of distinction has said that two qualities pervade American society to a degree of which Americans themselves are unaware — helpfulness and hope. These are frontier qualities. Settlers in a new country form the habit of standing together, and they always look forward to safety, comfort and prosperity. And in a country in which the frontier has only recently disappeared and in large sections of which the earliest generation of settlers is still represented, the habit of helpfulness and the spirit of hope are in the air.

Along the Atlantic seaboard the oldest communities have their social traditions, their well-defined social standards; but in these communities new groups of people are continually coming to the front, bringing with them a careless indifference to the imaginary social lines drawn by the descendants of the older families; the Central West, into whose hands the political control of the country has passed, and the Far West, steadily gaining weight in the direction of national affairs, are radically democratic. This does not mean that they refuse to recognize superiority of character or training, or that they are envious of the wealth of others; it means that they are bent on the preservation of a social order in which men shall be respected, not for what they inherit but for what they achieve; and that the paths to success shall be kept open. This determination to keep the doors open to industry and ability is one of the prime factors in the struggle now going on in America to make an end of special privileges and to keep a free field for individual effort. The fight is not against wealth, but against giving opportunities for acquiring wealth to a few instead of offering, as near as possible, the same opportunities to all.

"The treasury of America," President Wilson has recently said, "lies in those ambitions, those energies, that cannot be restricted to a special favored class. It depends upon the inventions of unknown men, upon the originations of unknown men, upon the ambitions of unknown men. Every country is renewed out of the ranks of the unknown, not out of the ranks of those already famous and powerful and in control." To keep the door of opportunity so easily moved that a touch of strength, of energy, of ability will set it wide is the settled determination of the Americans of to-day.

The average American resents the exploitation of wealth and the endeavor to create a social order on a property basis. He respects an aristocracy based on blood, though he refuses to regard it as constituting a basis for political privilege; but he resents the effort to establish a plutocracy. In a western community, where the democratic spirit is most pronounced, the man who has made a fortune fairly avoids vulgar display and is generous in his support of community interests, — is held in high respect as a citizen who is also a good neighbor. For neighborliness, which is helpfulness become habitual and practical, is almost a fetish in America. It has come down from the days when the little group of families on the frontier made a kind of common capital of their resources; fought together for the safety of their homes; worked together when their crops were threatened by sudden dangers; and in sickness or sorrow became one family. The average American is proud of the success of his neighbor; it reflects a certain credit on himself and on the community; but when the successful man remains in the neighborhood but ceases to be a neighbor, he becomes not envious of his wealth but offended by his selfish use of it.

Mr. Kipling has said that the French talk a great deal about liberty, equality and fraternity, but care only for equality; that the English hate equality and fraternity, but care greatly for liberty; that Americans are indifferent to liberty and equality, but insist on fraternity. And it is true that good-fellowship counts immensely in public regard in America. To be a "good-fellow," to have cordial manners, to keep a pleasant word ready, to be easy of access and always at hand with a cheerful temper and a willingness to help, is to have a wide latitude in the matter of personal conduct. The political "boss" understands this weakness in his countrymen and has organized "good-fellowship" into a system which the reformers find it hard to

AMERICAN IDEALS

overturn. He is so ready to serve his constituents that he seems to them an efficient servant of the community; when, as a matter of fact, his cordiality and helpfulness are simply political assets. He finds work for the unemployed, makes generous gifts of coal and flour when work and wages fail, supplies doctors and medicines in sickness, arranges excursions and dances for his supporters among the working classes, and stands before them as a friend in need on a great scale.

Many a corruptionist in American politics has held his place because he was known to be a devoted husband and father, a generous giver to churches and charities, and a man with a cordial grasp of the hand and a pleasant smile for all comers.

But this regard for the man of genial manners and readiness to help is the excess of one of the finest American qualities, neighborliness. In this respect America is a great village from the Atlantic to the Pacific, and what happens in Portland, Maine, greatly interests the people of Portland, Oregon. If there is an outbreak of yellow fever in some section of the

AMERICAN AND HIS GOVERNMENT

South, doctors and nurses are rushed to the point, by special train if necessary; if great floods bring widespread suffering in the Mississippi Valley, the whole nation opens its pocketbook; if Charleston is damaged by an earthquake, subscriptions for the benefit of the suffering are instantly forwarded; if a great fire sweeps a city, other cities stand ready to help it rebuild; when San Francisco was overtaken by a great calamity a few years ago, the nation rose as one man to help it. Cities, villages, boards of trade, churches, opened subscription lists, and $9,500,000 was sent at once, and more would have gone if the local committee of relief had not announced that no more money could be used to advantage. The nation thought of little else for weeks, and every kind of aid, public and private, was at the service of the stricken city. The whole country was neighbor to it.

The instinct that makes Americans jealous of any loss of this spirit of neighborliness is sound; for it is not only a deep spring of democratic feeling but a moderating and regulating influence in a country in which

AMERICAN IDEALS

individual initiative plays so great a part. It does not check individual energy but subdues it to common uses; redeems it from hard selfishness; and sweetens success by insisting that it shall be shared with the community.

There are men of immense wealth in America whose names have become symbols of business oppression, of unfair methods in crushing competitors, of lessening opportunities for young men with no other capital than character, energy and ability. They are disliked not because they are rich men — that is, in itself, a matter of indifference — but because they have not been good neighbors. To keep this spirit of generous sharing of opportunity, of mutual helpfulness, Americans are just now revising their laws, extending the authority of the National government and pledging themselves anew, in many practical ways, that the government of the people, by the people, for the people shall not perish from the face of the earth.

XI

COUNTRY AND PEOPLE

MUCH confusion of thought has been caused by the habit of speaking of peoples as if they were all cast in the same mold. We are so accustomed to the use of the phrase "the Japanese," "the English," "the Americans" that we have come to think of these words as definite and exact characterizations. Nothing could be more misleading; these peoples have certain physical characteristics which are the results of race and climate; they have certain racial forms of thought and speech; but they present differences of character and culture as marked as those which exist between alien races. It has taken Europe a long time to learn that there are Americans *and* Americans; and that the London cockney is not further removed in intelligence from the Englishman of university training than is the ignorant American from the man who, like Lowell, has the knowledge of the Old and the wit of the New World. In France the men of Normandy and of Brittany are Frenchmen, but in temperament and habit of thought they are farther apart than some Frenchmen and Italians.

America, like Japan, has several climates. In the Far North deep snow lies on the ground almost half the year; in the woods of Maine and Michigan the winter has an arctic severity. In the Far South the roses bloom in every month, and sea bathing is a recreation in January. On the New England coast when fogs and east winds are making men ask whether life is worth living, the everglades of Florida are brilliant with tropical flowers, and the sky of Southern California is cloudless.

And in these different environments different types of men have been bred. The New England type and the Southern type have been specially definite in their diversities and exceptionally influential in shaping the affairs of the country. New England was settled by men and women of resolute will, strong convictions, self-denying frugality

COUNTRY AND PEOPLE

and industry, with a great regard for education. The climate was rigorous and the soil exacting full payment in toil for every ounce of product. Family life was singularly pure and unworldly; integrity, self-reliance and the habit of work were fundamental in the education of children. Independence of judgment was carried to an extreme, and no section of the country has bred so many reformers and rebels against conventions, ready to stand alone if need be for a principle. In almost every New England village there will still be found a recluse, who lives by himself because he cannot make the compromise with absolute freedom which living with others would involve. The New Englander has been the founder of colleges, the organizer of churches, the leader of ethical movements.

In the South, on the other hand, the climate is milder, the soil more responsive. There is far more activity in the saddle and with the gun, and social life has filled a much larger place in the sum total of living. There has been less seriousness of spirit, though no less power of sacrifice. Manners have been more gracious, though they have expressed no greater readiness to help than the more restrained New Englander has felt. A more relaxed temper has made life less strenuous than in New England; and while religious faith has been more conservative its pressure on social habits has been more lightly borne.

The people of the West bear the impress of both sections, but have developed types of their own; they have the New England faith in education, but they have shaped their universities with a free hand to meet their own conditions; they stand together in all times of need and in all enterprises for the common benefit with uncalculating loyalty and generosity; they have the strong social instinct of the South, but they are far more democratic in spirit and habit. The somewhat rigid outlines of the New England type are blurred in the West, while the easy-going Southern habit is reënforced by fresh energy and the passion for success. Manners are unconventionally cordial.

The landscape of the country is on a vast scale and presents certain broad divisions

COUNTRY AND PEOPLE

which have played their part in the development of the nation. The Atlantic seaboard is a long stretch of comparatively level and arable country from Maine in the North to Florida at the South. In this belt are the older cities and communities; the stubborn but well-worked farms of New England; the broad fertility of New York and Pennsylvania; the garden-like fruit farms of Delaware and Maryland; the naturally productive soil of Virginia, and the rice and cotton fields of South Carolina. At the back of this long stretch of comparatively level strip of country rises a range of mountains running from North to South, and, in the earlier days, forming a formidable barrier to the growth of the colonies westward. From the western slope of these mountains there stretches a vast tract of country which the Mississippi and its tributaries first opened to the world; an empire within the continent; a thousand miles and more of fertile soil which was once largely prairie country and is now a vast community of farms with large and intensely active cities as distributing centers. Where the prairies

AMERICAN IDEALS

— level, fertile and, in the spring, radiant with flowers — end the plains begun, at a much higher altitude and with a colder and dryer climate. They were formerly ranges over which wild cattle roamed; later domesticated cattle were driven hither and thither over a great stretch of unoccupied country which is now made fertile by irrigation and divided into great cattle farms. This tract of country still in the early stages of development ends at the foothills of the Rocky Mountains, which traverse the continent from North to South, and slope westward to the Pacific.

An American artist of distinction has said of the noble figure of Buddha at Kamakura: "It is not a little thing made big, like our modern colossal statues; it has always been big, and would be so if reduced to life size." The figure, in other words, is not simply large; it is great. It was conceived on a great scale and was executed with a commensurate boldness and power. Size of itself is not significant; it may be mere extension of surface, a vast landscape without composition.

COUNTRY AND PEOPLE

There is a radical difference between size and scale. America is not simply a large country; it is, speaking geographically, a great country, a country fashioned on a great scale. If the continent is studied in elevation, it will show diversities of structure — composition, as the painters would call it—as clearly as Japan, Italy or England. It is not, as some people seem to imagine, a vast monotony of prairie and plain; it is a continent of manifold diversities of landscape.

The scale on which the country is molded is an element which has deeply impressed the imagination of the people from the beginning and has deeply affected their history. Bryant, the earliest American poet of importance, gave his verse an elemental quality and conveyed a sense of the mystery which inheres in vastness. It may be that the tendency to moralization, which Dr. Nitobe has noted in the closing lines of the fine verses "To a Waterfowl," and which he rightly says no Japanese poet would have felt it necessary to add, was a refuge from the almost overwhelming sense of vastness on the American continent. In the presence of a landscape of such extent and majesty men of imagination are driven to offset the mass or weight of earth with assertions of the supremacy of the spirit. And it is a significant fact about American literature that its notes have been idealistic and altruistic; it has lacked so far the solidity and physical basis, so to speak, of the older literatures, but it has had notable purity of tone and elevation of thought. On the bleak New England coasts in the days of the first migration, on the level sweep of prairie country in the time of the second migration, on the edges of the Grand Canyon or in the lonely gorges of the Rocky Mountains or of the Sierra Nevadas to-day, men take refuge from the sense of insignificance in the assertion of their spiritual superiority.

The scale on which the continent is molded has laid on Americans a task of almost crushing magnitude. The work of exploration and settlement, begun almost three centuries ago, is still incomplete. The transcontinental railways were constructed by men many of

COUNTRY AND PEOPLE

whom are still living, and the disappearance of the frontier is a matter of the last ten years; frontier conditions still continue in large sections of the country, and vast tracts of land are still to be settled and developed. The work of settlement has involved continuous toil and almost continuous danger; and the foundations of every new community have been laid in self-denial, self-sacrifice, heroic work and indomitable hope. Americans have been criticized for the slowness with which their art has developed; but their critics forget the preoccupation of a task of colossal magnitude, the absorption of energy and strength involved in reclaiming a continent and converting it into three thousand miles of practically continuous farms; with the building of roads, making of tools and creation of governmental, educational and social institutions, which have been involved in this development.

Emerson has said in effect that the most valuable product of a farm is not crops but character, and that men take out of the earth much more than they put into it. The con-

AMERICAN IDEALS

version of a continent into a home has largely shaped American character and must be taken into account in any study of their life. It has exalted work into something like a religion; it has discredited the idler; it has awakened the active qualities and stimulated self-reliance, self-respect and the passion for personal independence. In every country the owners of land have great influence; in America they form a very large proportion of the population, and the able men who are the managers of the business of the country from offices and banks in the cities are largely drawn from those who were born on farms. The productivity of the American farms for 1912 was nine billion five hundred million dollars, an increase of about one hundred and forty per cent during the last fifteen years. And now that scientific methods of farming are being introduced, and the betterment of agriculture has become part of the business of the government, under the direction of experts, it is impossible to predict the wealth-producing capacity of American farms in the near future. The pro-

COUNTRY AND PEOPLE

duction of coal, iron, oil, copper, silver has shown a commensurate increase. Americans are often accused of boasting because they quote such stupendous figures in describing the resources of the country; but it is impossible to ignore these figures, because they are of great significance in the life of the country. They mean not only wealth but energy, ability, opportunity, a heavy tax on time and thought and strength.

To the charge that he is vulgarly rich the American might plead his inability to escape wealth because he has inherited an estate which is so enormously productive; he has shown only the sagacity which other active races would have shown under the same conditions. Those conditions have laid a task on his shoulders which has absorbed his energy and strength for a century and has drawn from the direct service of the State many men of ability who, in other countries, would have been political leaders. In America public life, as has been pointed out, is not synonymous with politics; it is shared by all men and women who contribute largely to the general welfare : heads of colleges, philanthropists, men of affairs, builders of railroads, organizers of industry. There are in America men of affairs who have shown the daring that in the sixteenth century would have made them great explorers and adventurers, the imagination that would have made them poets, the breadth of view and the sense of things to come that in other countries would have made them statesmen.

It sometimes happens that the heir to a vast property is compelled to devote the earlier years of his possession to the organization and development of his estate; other interests may call him loudly and his heart may respond to their call, but for the moment his work confronts him with such urgency of demand that to leave it undone would be to turn his back on that which Carlyle declared has the supreme claim on a man — the duty that lies next him.

The charge of materialism, which has become the stock in trade of many critics of American society, is largely made, as is most

COUNTRY AND PEOPLE

criticism of nations by foreign observers, from a very superficial knowledge of conditions. It may not be a matter of credit to America that it has become a very rich country, and it is certainly true that some Americans have obtruded that fact on the attention of the world too insistently; but it is a matter of simple justice to remember that if America had failed to develop the resources of the continent, the same critics would have put her among those races which either fall a prey to more energetic peoples or furnish standard illustrations of national inefficiency.

The sense of still greater possibilities of development pervades the air of America and finds expression in the speech, the imagination, the temperament of the people. An American artist, on the wall of a library building, has striven to represent the spirit of the people by a procession of men, women and children. They are all marching together, with eager expectation on their upturned faces, and the morning light shines on them. It was a happy inspiration to paint hope, not as an allegorical figure, but as an impulse

AMERICAN IDEALS

which is like martial music to a moving host. In America the future is not an indefinite apprehension; it is an ardent expectation: a promise not only of ample prosperity but of a fuller, more interesting, more satisfying life.

And so the thought of the American to-day centers more and more on the well-being of the coming generation; on the protection of women and children from oppressive working hours and unwholesome industrial conditions; on securing cleanliness, light and air in the homes of the poor; educational opportunities ample enough for those who want the most thorough technical training and for those who must begin at an early age to care for themselves; the husbanding of the resources of the country for the benefit of future generations. Americans have been prodigal givers of land, forests, mines, water power; they have surrendered to private enterprises sources of great public revenue. They have now reversed this spendthrift policy; henceforth, these resources will be developed and managed by private hands on generous

COUNTRY AND PEOPLE

terms; but a proper return will be required in order that the national property may bear its share of the national expenses.

The pressure of work which must be done at once necessarily involved much provisional building of houses and railroads in the country, and has compelled the almost universal rebuilding which is going on in all sections. The same pressure of work and the extent of the territory to be covered have made carelessness, even slovenliness, far too prevalent in America, in most parts of which the neatness which characterizes England and Belgium, for instance, is conspicuously lacking. Here again the element of scale and the shortness of time in which the work has been done must be taken into account.

The impress of scale is seen not only in American aims and character but in its art and literature. In American books there is a new kind of passion for Nature; not the exquisite Greek sense of detail which makes Theocritus both the poet and the natural historian of Sicily; not Wordsworth's mystical feeling of the presence of the soul suffusing the world with intimations of immortality; not the sensitive response of Tennyson to the elusive and fleeting no less than to the obvious aspect of a world grown familiar with use and intimate through toil and sorrow; but a sense of the vastness, sublimity and loneliness of Nature; the detachment of a landscape not yet humanized by cultivation and by paths across the fields. Fuji, the Incomparable, rises uncompanioned into the lonely sky, a vast altar set afar in unbroken silence; the highest peaks in America rise out of great ranges of hills, in a landscape so vast that they can be approached only with peril and hardship. If the "Lines on Tintern Abbey" are compared with Lanier's "Marshes of Glynn," or the companionable notebook of White of Selbourne with Thoreau's "Maine Woods," or Jefferies' "Wild Life in a Southern County" with Mr. Burroughs' records of Nature in America, the difference in scale between a small and highly cultivated country like England and a vast and still largely uncultivated country like the United States will stand out with striking distinctness.

COUNTRY AND PEOPLE

Nor does the influence of the scale of resources end with a report of its effect on temperament and achievement; it must be reckoned with in any attempt to understand the financial development of the last forty years. These four decades of growth and prosperity have brought with them temptations to the abuse of success to which the men of no other race have been subjected. The population has grown from thirty-eight and a half millions in 1870 to ninety-three or four millions in 1912. Three years ago the wealth of the country was estimated at $142,000,000,-000. These figures are not quoted because they afford any standard of national ability or any measure of national greatness; but simply because they suggest the strain to which the government of the United States and the American character have been subjected. They do not justify boasting, and to-day there is very little inclination in America to print them in large letters on the title page of current history; nor, on the other hand, are they to be apologized for. A nation, like an individual, is not called upon to explain events or experiences which have been beyond its control. It is true, Americans have not neglected the business which has fallen into their hands, but it is also true that Nature, the silent partner in the American enterprise, has furnished the capital and the material from which the tools have been made. In no other country, in so short a time, has such an immense acreage of fertility been opened and such an army of workers responded to the call of opportunity.

The result has been a stimulation of business activity which has intoxicated many men of naturally sober temper. When a great crop is to be gathered in and the weather is uncertain, men work, not only overtime but all the time. In the United States a flood tide of prosperity found the old channels of law and method inadequate, and men have been swept along without any clear realization of the speed with which they were moving. The necessity of handling efficiently the details of enormous business operations and of using vast sums of money has brought into existence combinations of a magnitude undreamed of in

COUNTRY AND PEOPLE

the earlier history of the country and the radical effects of which in restricting competition and diminishing individual opportunity were foreseen neither by lawmakers nor by financiers; and the country has slowly awakened to the fact that it must devise some working basis for vast wealth in a few hands in a democratic society.

In this rushing tide of activity some men have been swept from their moral moorings, and the speculative and gambling spirit, which is always stimulated by universal prosperity and from which all countries have suffered, has tempted some men to unscrupulous use of wealth and to downright dishonesty; but the fact that the credit system is the basis of enormous transactions and that, while it is sometimes extended beyond the limits of safety, it is so rarely abused that the confidence of the country in the fundamental integrity of the business community is never seriously disturbed, and that the percentage of loss in handling enormous investments and trust funds is so small as to be almost negligible, furnish the best possible evidence of the soundness of American business men. The finances of the government from the beginning have been managed with conspicuous integrity and the losses through the dishonesty of government officials have been so small that they may be ignored.

Whoever reads the report of corporate oppression in the United States during the last four decades and does not take into account the swift and unparalleled increase in wealth, not only does a great injustice to the country, but fails to understand the situation as completely as Gladstone and Carlyle failed to understand the War between the States fifty years ago.

This prosperity has not gone wholly into luxury, though it has increased the cost of living in America and has led to great elaboration of what may be called the machinery of living, to extravagance and to display; it has endowed education and scientific investigation on a scale unprecedented in the history of education. To some of these gifts the American public, always quick to see the humorous aspects of current events, has

COUNTRY AND PEOPLE

taken a somewhat cynical attitude and has plainly hinted that some gifts to colleges and universities have been attempts at restitution, and that the multimillionaire of to-day who endows a university is the modern successor of the medieval baron who, after pillaging a city and putting its innocent inhabitants to the sword, made his peace with Heaven by building a church. There is as much human nature in America as there is in England, Germany or Japan, and there is the same partial application of ideals to action as in these older countries; but the most obvious interest of the American, according to the most capable observers, is his interest in education. It is one of the expressions of his faith in the future which is shared by men of all stations in life. The gifts of private persons are on a great scale, the appropriations of states and cities are on the same scale; the citizen expects to give his children every educational advantage within his means; and in America, as in Japan, no sacrifice is too great to send the boy to college and the university. The newly arrived immigrant in

AMERICAN IDEALS

America does not rest until his children are in the schools. Many foreigners think the magic phrase in America is "getting on"; but they are mistaken; that phrase is a compact description of the prosperity which is, in the minds of men and women who have children to guide, a basis for "getting up." It is a kind of national tradition, even among men who have made great fortunes with little aid from education, that children must have larger opportunities than their parents and that in point of opportunity each generation must stand on the shoulders of the generation which precedes it.

For among Americans education is not only a discipline, a training; it is also a symbol. It stands for the larger freedom which political liberty foreshadows; it means living an ampler life in a larger world. It is one form of that practical idealism, that passion for human betterment, which sent a host of men and women to the New World for conscience' sake; men and women who opened schools and founded colleges before they were safely housed in the wilderness, and have

COUNTRY AND PEOPLE

continued to build schools and colleges as fast as they advanced the frontier toward the Pacific.

They have also built churches, for religion has been one of the major motives in American civilization; a symbol of idealism and a rule of life; and the church has been a center of social and altruistic activity. In every village there is a substantial church building; often more than are justified by the population; and there is an academy or high school. Puritanism in the New England colonies was not only a form of faith but a political order as well; membership in the church was a qualification for voting. The contemporaries of Milton and Cromwell held their faith with an intensity of conviction which tolerated no differences of opinion. But before the adoption of the Constitution the religious tests had been abolished and freedom of worship recognized as a fundamental right of every citizen. There is no principle which Americans hold more tenaciously than this, nor is there one which they guard with more vigilance. Every attempt to use public funds for sectarian purposes or to secure government aid for such purpose is met by a storm of protest. The government stands absolutely neutral in its relation to religion, and the separation of the State from the Church is complete. The name of the Supreme Being does not occur in the Constitution, and government institutions of all kinds are entirely free from control by any kind of ecclesiastical organization.

The American people have always been and are to-day a religious people. They formed the habit early in their history of suspending business one day in seven, and of keeping Sunday not only as a day of rest but as a day of worship; and, while they have ceased to be Sabbatarians in the rigid sense and have come to believe that the Sabbath was made for man and not man for the Sabbath, they still guard the freedom of the day from the intrusion of all business which is not necessary for human safety and comfort, and they attend religious services in large numbers. They have no possession of greater value from a religious or domestic point of view or as a means of public health, of wholesome out-of-

COUNTRY AND PEOPLE

door life, of the rest that "reknits the ravelled sleeve of care," and gives workers of all kinds renewal of energy, than the weekly holiday which their ancestors, for two thousand years, have set aside for the things of the spirit. One of their wisest thinkers has touched the secret of the Sunday peace which falls on the rushing industrial life of America and is dear to Americans of every creed in these eloquent words: When the seventh day dawns, white with the worship of uncounted centuries, "the cathedral music of history breathes through it a psalm to our solitude." Like a quiet path, through which all one's ancestors have walked, this day, set apart to rest and worship, runs back to the far beginnings of Christian civilization and is one of its most precious gifts to the world.

A majority of the people of the United States have some religious connection, and the churches are the center of devotional, charitable and altruistic activity of many kinds. Professor Münsterberg, a critical student of American conditions, has said that "the entire American people are in fact profoundly religious, and have been, from the day when the Pilgrim Fathers landed, down to the present moment." In nearly every document which conveyed authority to discoverers, explorers and settlers in the New World the Christian religion was recognized, and in a decision rendered in 1891 by the Supreme Court of the United States these words are found: "If we pass beyond these matters to a view of American life as expressed by its laws, its business, its customs and its society, we find everywhere a clear recognition of the same truth. Among other matters note the following: The form of oath universally prevailing, concluding with an appeal to the Almighty; the custom of opening sessions of all deliberate bodies with prayer; the prefatory words of all wills: 'In the name of God, Amen'; the laws respecting the observance of the Sabbath with a general cessation of all secular business, and the closing of courts, legislatures and similar public assemblies on that day; the churches and church organizations which abound in every city, town and hamlet; the multitude of charitable organiza-

COUNTRY AND PEOPLE

tions existing everywhere under Christian auspices; the gigantic missionary associations, with general support, and aiming to establish Christian Missions in every quarter of the globe. These and many other matters which might be noticed add a volume of unofficial declarations to the mass of organic utterances that this is a Christian nation."

In the American temperament, in spite of its practical energy and consuming activity, there is a deep spring of idealism which has so far found inadequate expression in art, but has been an abundant source of national inspiration in religious activity, education and practical helpfulness. The division of Christian people into sects, the rigid definitions which their faith has often had in terms of traditional theology, the intense feeling with which creeds have been not only held but imposed upon others, the rapid spread of crude mysticism combined with empirical uses, the attraction of a bald literalism for half-educated people, are the excesses, the one-sided expressions, of a deep and lasting interest in the ultimate questions of human destiny. In the busiest of countries there is one question which is never silenced — the question of immortality.

The religious attitude of the American, which was once largely subjective is now largely objective; and the test of faith is no longer the acceptance of a definition but some form of service of humanity. There are certain facts which as a believer in a historical religion the Christian in America holds as fundamental, but the value of a man's religion is estimated in terms of social service. The Puritan emphasis on conduct as the only convincing evidence of the religious spirit makes itself felt more distinctly to-day than ever before in the history of the country; but the weight of that emphasis has been transferred from the individual to society, and the impulse which is stirring Americans as they have not been stirred since the war which ended fifty years ago, and which is behind the leading political parties, is the determination to make industrial and social conditions conform to the standards of Christian ethics. Seventeenth-century Puritanism

COUNTRY AND PEOPLE

insisted that a man should save his own soul; twentieth-century Puritanism insists that he shall save society by creating conditions which shall help men to live wholesome lives as human beings.

There has been no more generous and unselfish example of the desire of the American to give the world the best he has than the missionary movement, which took an organized form in Williams College one hundred and seven years ago; a noble adventure in faith and service which has made the world familiar with the highest types of American character; an organized friendship of the spirit which has translated the great words "Peace on earth and good will to men" into all languages.

The country has always been the home of the reforming spirit, and in their most comfortable days Americans have never been satisfied. They grew restive under the existence of slavery, which was carried to America at a time when it was accepted as a normal condition in the greater part of the world; they finally destroyed it by an immense sacrifice of life and property. They

AMERICAN IDEALS

have not yet succeeded in solving the difficult problem of controlling the manufacture and sale of intoxicating liquor, but they have never ceased to make experiments and they have won the fight in many of the states. For many years a vigorous agitation was conducted against Mormonism until the plural marriage was heavily penalized. It is impossible to open an American newspaper without reading reports of the proceedings of some organization to protect women and children from industrial oppression, to open schools in the slums, to build or endow hospitals, to secure playgrounds for children; in a word, in manifold ways to make life more wholesome and happy for the less fortunate and helpless members of society. The American who does not belong to half a dozen organizations of this kind and is not working on half a dozen committees is a rare person. The country is ravaged by societies formed to do good to somebody; men of means, large or small, are besieged with appeals for money for charitable uses, for education, for public purposes. In 1912 the amount given by

COUNTRY AND PEOPLE

individuals for education, for religious uses, for general beneficence, not including provisions of all kinds for the poor, exceeded, according to a report reprinted in a Tokyo newspaper, $315,000,000. There have been humorous proposals to organize a society for the suppression of philanthropy and reform; but Americans are every year giving more time and money for altruistic uses.

One of the ablest American politicians has said that if a political movement assumes a moral aspect, nothing can resist it. The one appeal which arouses enthusiasm in Americans to-day is the ethical appeal, and the men who are now the leaders of public opinion are teachers of public morals. Those who have not understood the tasks laid on Americans in making a home for men and women of all races in the New World, nor the temptations which have assailed them, have so often repeated the charge that Americans are materialists that Europe has fallen into the habit of automatically reiterating a phrase which, to one who understands the temper of the people of the United States, is not only mis-

AMERICAN IDEALS

leading, but a caricature of the American spirit. What makes a man a materialist? Not dealing with material substances and forms and physical forces, for the vast majority of men spend their lives in patient toil with the stubborn stuff in which and with which the whole world works. One does not call the architect a materialist because he handles enormous masses of stone or iron, or the painter a materialist because he is soiled with pigments, or the musician a materialist because he uses instruments of wood and ivory and metal. A materialist is a man who works with materials and is satisfied with them; whose soul is colored by the things in which he deals, "like the dyer's hand," to recall Shakespeare. Those who know America know that it is a national peculiarity to be satisfied with nothing. Americans are not discontented, but they are dissatisfied; they always want something better than they possess; they are eager to get the best life offers; as soon as they get money, they want education, opportunities of travel, art.

They are charged with the willingness to

COUNTRY AND PEOPLE

sell their souls for money,—a kind of barter which is extensively carried on in all parts of the world. But Americans care far less for money than many other races. The attractions of business on a great scale for the energetic American is the opportunity of putting forth his full strength, of matching himself against obstacles and overcoming them, of measuring his ability against the ability of competitors; the excitement of playing the game interests him more than winning the stakes. When money in large quantities comes into his hands he does not hoard it; misers are almost unknown in America; he spends it freely; he often lavishes it on his family, and harms his children by his unwise generosity; he gives it away in increasing amounts. The great fortunes which have subjected him to sharp criticism in America have made vast contributions to public uses.

Contrary to the opinion based on the traditional ignorance of American conditions which is now slowly yielding to the pressure of knowledge, the American is very emotional and governed largely by sentiment. The terrible struggle between the States, in which nearly 800,000 men were killed or wounded, and the cost of which was probably not less than $4,000,000,000, not including the destruction of slave property in the South to the extent of $2,000,000,000, showed that when sentiment is involved, the Americans do not count the cost. That is one of the qualities which reveal the ineradicable and controlling idealism which has been a dominating element in America since the first colonists braved the dangers of a new world for conscience' sake. That idealism has not yet found adequate expression in their art; but it has shaped American institutions. The government is the most daring credit system the world has ever known; it rests on the assumption that men without regard to education or social condition can be trusted with the management of the most important affairs of life.

Americans have regarded their freedom and their opportunities as a trust for humanity and have shared them with men and women

COUNTRY AND PEOPLE

of the whole western world. They have made provision for universal education; they have responded to every appeal for aid from other nations in times of calamity; their fleet went instantly to the rescue of Messina, and they organized rebuilding on a large scale; they bore the burden of a war to give Cuba her freedom; the story of their diplomacy in Japan and China need not be rehearsed here; their service to the Philippines is recognized by every traveler; to-day they have undertaken to reorganize their business so as to bring it into accord with the spirit of their institutions and with the Christian ethics they profess. Their faults are recorded in the newspapers of the world. They do not ask for charity of judgment; they must be judged by what they have done and are trying to do under the circumstances in which they have been placed; and their tendency to take a cheerful view of things induces them to hope that the world will sometime take the trouble to understand these circumstances. Whether it does or does not, the Americans will continue to strive to achieve a solution not only

AMERICAN IDEALS

of the political problem, which Matthew Arnold declared they had solved, but of the human problem, which is infinitely more complex and difficult, and for which no race or nation has yet found a final solution.

INDEX

A

Adams, Herbert, portrait busts by, 209.
Adams, John, literary work of, 109.
Adams, John Quincy, President and Harvard professor, 246.
Adams, Samuel, defense of rights of Americans written by, 107.
Advanced work in American universities, 257 ff.
Albany Capitol, paintings by W. M. Hunt in the, 199-200.
Aldrich, Thomas Bailey, tribute to work of, 185.
Allen, James Lane, literary art of, 175.
Allston, Washington, 196.
America, misunderstanding of, by foreigners, 6-7; fundamental differences between political and social structure and that of older countries, 13 ff.; significance of discovery of, 39-40; the settlement of, 42-60; colonies of, experiment stations in science of government, 61 ff.; mistaken policy in management of colonies of, 62-67; condition of, at time colonists won independence, 68-70; political organization formulated for, 70-81, 274 ff.; development of the continent by the new nation, 81-90; literature of, in provincial period, 91-127; sectional literature of, 128-155; national literature of, following War between the States, 156 ff.; architecture in, 189-194; progress in painting in, 194-203; sculpture in, 203-210; music in, 210-213; education and life in school and college, 214-244; universities of, 245-257; opportunities for advanced and research work, 257-266; as the land of opportunity, 285-290; qualities of neighborliness and good-fellowship in, 290-294; effects of different climates and environments of, 296-298; influence of vastness of landscape, 298 ff.
Americanisms, origins of phrases called, 98-99.
"American Political Ideas," quoted, 75-76.
Americans, interest and admiration felt by, for the Japanese nation, 1-2; possibility of interpretation of, by an American writer, 11-12; attitude of, toward education, 14-16, 23-25, 214 ff., 316; political institutions favored by, 17-18; suitability of form of government to, 18-19; consciousness of perils of system, 19-20; risks of misrepresentation and misunderstanding felt by, 20-23;

INDEX

talking and writing by, without preparation, 26 ff.; newspapers of, and wrong impressions given by, 28–33; racial strains in composition of, 42–60, 267–269; clinging of, to the English language, 96–99; literary foundations of, 99–102; advance of the national spirit among, resulting from the War between the States, 154, 156; trait of individual initiative in, 281; self-reliance of, 281–283; unlimited opportunities for, 285–287; qualities of helpfulness and hope, 288; neighborliness and good-fellowship supreme among qualities of, 290–294; varieties of, with variations in climate and environment, 295–300; effect of great scale of country upon, 300 ff.; explanation of charge of materialism brought against, 306; attitude toward religion, 317–323; the reforming spirit among, 323–325; emotion and sentiment of, 327–328; the promise of further progress by, 328–330.

Andover, academy at, 225.

Architecture, colonial, 189–190; chaotic period following War between the States, 190–194; modern improvement in, 194.

Arnold, Matthew, quoted, 115, 330.

Athletics, interest in, at American colleges, 238–243.

"Autobiography," Franklin's, 118.

Automobiles, as a means of national development, 158–159.

"Awakening of Helena Richie," 181.

B

Ball, Thomas, work in sculpture by, 208.

Baltimore, the Lords, 56.

Bancroft, George, 127, 170.

Bartlett, the "Lafayette" and "Genius of Man" of, 209.

"Bathers," W. M. Hunt's, 199.

"Battle Hymn of the Republic, The," 154.

Beaux, Cecilia, 203.

Berea College, 283.

Bible, results of translation of, 45–47; as a vitalizing power with American colonists, 101–102.

"Biglow Papers," Lowell's, 138.

Blair, James, 218.

"Blithedale Romance," Hawthorne's, 144.

Books of early American settlers, 94–96.

Boston, music in, 212.

Boston Latin School, 217.

"Boy and the Butterfly," W. M. Hunt's, 199.

Boyle, "Stone Age" of, 209.

"Bracebridge Hall," Irving's, 122.

Brewster, William, 94.

Bringhurst, "Kiss of Eternity" of, 209–210.

Brown, Charles Brockden, 145.

Brownell, critical essays by, 186–187.

Brunetière, on American distances, 157.

Bryant, William Cullen, discussion of work of, 128, 133–135; influence of vast scale of America on poetry of, 301–302.

Bryce, James, on the American Constitution, 74; on the West of America, 83.

332

INDEX

Bryn Mawr College, 237.
Buddha, thoughts inspired by figure of, 300.
Burroughs, John, 186; nature writing of, contrasted with that of Jefferies, 310.
Butler, Nicholas Murray, on the Puritan strain in Americans, 50–51.

C

Cable, George W., 175.
Cabot, John, 40.
California, discovery of gold in, 89.
Carnegie Endowment for International Peace, 265–266.
Carnegie Foundation for the Advancement of Teaching, 263–264.
Carnegie Institution of Washington, 262.
Carolinas, settlement of the, 57–58.
"Certain Rich Man," White's, 181.
"Chanting Cherubs," Greenough's, 204.
Chatham, Lord, 109.
Chicago, University of, age of, 249; endowment of, 250.
Children, American poetry which appeals to, 135–136.
Civil War, the American, 8, 153, 158.
Clark University, 254; teaching of pedagogy at, 258–259.
Clemens, Samuel N., 176.
Cleveland, Grover, 15.
Climate, effect of, on people in different sections of America, 296–298.
Colby, Frank, 186.

Colleges, the first American, 217 ff.; courses and system of education in, 226 ff.; elective system in, 232–234; for women, 236–238; devotion to sports and athletics at, 238–242; social life at, 242–244.
Colonial system, mistakes of the old, 61–67.
Columbia University, gradual development and present size and endowment of, 249–250; School of Mines at, 258; Teachers College at, 258.
Columbus, Christopher, 40.
Comenius, Bishop, quotation from, 227.
"Commemoration Ode," Lowell's, 137.
Commerce, early, between Europe and Asia, 36–38.
Commissioner of Education, national, 223.
Composers, American, 213.
"Conquest of Granada," Irving's, 122, 169.
Constitution, the Federal, 74–77; debates and discussion preceding the, 112; form of government created by, 275–276.
Continental Congress, the, 69.
Cooper, J. F., career and work of, 144–148.
Copley, John, 194, 196.
Cosmopolitan life, fiction dealing with, 177–178.
Cotton gin, invention of the, 83.
Crothers, Samuel McChord, 186.

D

Dallin, "Signal of Peace" of, 209.
Distances in America, Brunetière on supposed effects of, 157.

333

INDEX

"Dixie," song, 155.
Dutch, contribution of, to American citizenship and ideals, 51-55.
Dvořák, New World Symphony of, 213.

E

Education, attitude of Americans as a nation toward, 14-16, 23-25, 214 ff.; National Bureau of, 223; endowments for encouraging advanced, 262-266; gifts of the wealthy to, 314-315; viewed by Americans as a symbol of the larger freedom, 316-317.
Edwards, Jonathan, 115-116.
Elective system in colleges, 232-234; reasons for introduction, 256.
Eliot, Charles W., 246-247.
Elwell, "Ceres" and "Kronos" of, 209.
Emerson, Ralph Waldo, 15; literary production of, 138-139; on America as the country of opportunity, 285.
England, influence of universities of, on American colleges, 238-239, 254-255, 256-257.
English language, American settlers and the, 96-98.
Essay, the, in modern American literature, 186-187.
"Evangeline," Longfellow's, 125.
Everett, Edward, 127, 246.
Exeter, academy at, 225.

F

Farmers, increasing importance of American, 304-305.
Farragut, Saint Gaudens' statue of, 207.

Federalist party, 79.
Federalist, The, 113.
Fichte, quoted, 8.
Fiction, writers of modern, 172-182.
Financial development of America, 311.
Fiske, John, 172.
Foster, Stephen, 212.
Foundations for research work and for endowment of higher education, 262-266.
Fox, Charles James, 109.
Fox, John, Jr., 176.
Franklin, Benjamin, 15, 73, 106; "Autobiography" of, 118.
"Freedom of the Will," Edwards', 116.
Freedom of worship in America, 317-318.
Freeman, Mary Wilkins, 177.
French, Daniel, 209.
French and Indian War, 106.
French ideals and methods in University of Virginia, 220.
Fulton, Robert, 82.

G

Garland, Hamlin, 177.
General Education Board, work of, 263.
George III and the American colonies, 65-67.
Georgia, types of native character furnished to fiction by, 176.
Germany, influence of thought and literature of, on American culture, 126-127; influence of, on American universities, 254-257.
Gladstone, W. E., Morley quoted on, 8.
Goethe, quoted, 4.

INDEX

Good-fellowship, American regard for, 290-292.
Government, bases of the American, 267 ff.; form of political organization, 274-276.
Great American Desert, 87-88.
"Greek Slave," Powers', 204.
Greenough, "Chanting Cherubs" of, 204.
Groton School, 225.
Group system of study in colleges, 234.

H

Hall, G. Stanley, 259.
Hamilton, Alexander, 17-18, 73; great services of, to American government, 77 ff.; contributions of, to debates out of which the Constitution grew, 112-113.
Hampton Institute, 283.
Harris, Joel Chandler, 176.
Harte, Bret, 176.
Harvard, John, library of, 95; founding of Harvard College by, 217.
Harvard College, founding of, 217-218; the multitude of courses at, 235; significance of word "university" as applied to, 253-254.
Hawthorne, Nathaniel, contribution of, to American literature, 141-145.
Henry, Patrick, 110.
Herrick, Robert, 177.
"Hiawatha," Longfellow's, 125.
High School, place of, in American scheme of education, 224-225.
Hill School, the, 225.
Historical literature, growth of, 168-172.

Holmes, O. W., literary production of, 139-140.
Homer, Winslow, 202.
"House of Mirth, The," 180.
"House of the Seven Gables," 144.
Howells, William Dean, 178, 179-180.
"Huckleberry Finn," 176.
Hudson, Henry, 52.
Hudson River School of painting, so called, 197.
Huguenots in America, 54-55, 58; in and about New York City, 120.
Hunt, William Morris, 199-200.

I

Idealism found in the American temperament, 321.
"Indian Hunter," Ward's, 207.
Indians in the West, 89-90; schools for, 222.
Inness, George, 198.
Institute of Technology, Boston, 258.
"Iron Woman, The," 181.
Irving, Washington, 121-123; historical work of, 169.
Italy, part played by, in early discovery and exploration, 39.

J

James, Henry, 177, 179, 180.
Japan, interest in and admiration felt by Americans for, 1-2; difficulty experienced by foreigners in understanding, 5-6; interpretation of people of, by Japanese writers, 11; conformability of government of, to

INDEX

genius of its people, 18; politeness a matter of national discipline in, 22; richness of, in proverbs, 99; relations between business and science recognized in educational scheme of, 229; effect of training in "team play" shown by, 242.
Jarvis, John Wesley, quoted concerning early painters, 195–196.
Jefferson, Thomas, 79, 109, 113–114; University of Virginia founded by, 220.
Jewett, Sarah Orne, 177.
Johns Hopkins University, Sidney Lanier at, 164; study of contemporary history at, 171; age of, 249; establishment of, by private endowment, 250; significance of word "university" as applied to, 254.
Johnson, Eastman, 202.
"Journal," Woolman's, 117–118.
Journalism in America, 28–33.
Jumel Mansion, New York, 190.

K

Kindergartens, education in, 222.
Kipling, Rudyard, on certain national traits, 291.

L

"Lady Baltimore," Wister's, 181.
La Farge, John, 200–201.
Lamb, Charles, 4.
Land, gifts of, for educational purposes, 222–223; influence of owners of, 304–305.
Landscape, effect of vastness of, on American character, 133–134, 298 ff.

Lanier, Sidney, career and work of, 164–167; contrast between nature verse of, and that of Wordsworth, 310.
Lawrenceville School, 225.
Leatherstocking Tales, Cooper's, 147–148.
"Legend of Sleepy Hollow," 123.
Lehigh University, 254, 258.
Leland Stanford University, establishment of, by private endowment, 250.
Libraries of early American settlers, 94–96.
"Life of Columbus," Irving's, 122.
"Life on the Mississippi," Mark Twain's, 176.
Lincoln, Abraham, 15; training possessed by, for the Presidency, 24; statue of, in Capitol, Washington, 206; statues in Lincoln Park, Chicago, and Rock Creek Cemetery, Washington, 207–208.
Liquor question, the, 324.
Locke, John, scheme of government of, 57.
Longfellow, H. W., 123–127.
Lopez, "Sprinter" of, 209.
Louisiana Purchase, the, 82.
Lowell, James Russell, on Thomas Jefferson, 109; consideration of career and literary work of, 136–137; on the object of college education, 228; an example of the educational leader as a public man, 246.

M

McMaster, John Bach, 172.
Macmonnies, work of, 209.

336

INDEX

MacNeil, "Sun Vow" of, 209.
"Madam Delphine," Cable's, 175.
Madison, James, 44, 73, 113.
Manual training in schools, 224.
"Marble Faun," Hawthorne's, 143.
Mark Twain, 176.
"Mars Chan," Page's, 175.
Marshall, John, 44, 80–81.
"Marshes of Glynn," Lanier's, 166; contrasted with "Lines on Tintern Abbey," 310.
Martin, Homer D., 198, 199.
"Maryland, My Maryland," 154.
Maryland, settlement of, 56–57.
Materialism, charge of, brought against Americans, 306–307; misleading nature of charge of, 325–326.
Matthews, Brander, 186.
"Meh Lady," Page's, 175.
Mercersberg Academy, 225.
Mexican War, the, 89.
Military Academy, United States, 223.
Missionary movement, the, 323.
Monuments, shocking American, 191–192.
Moody, W. V., 185.
Morley, John, quoted, 8.
Mormonism, agitation against, 324.
Motley, J. L., 169–170.
Mt. Holyoke College, 237.
Mount Vernon, architecture of, 190.
Münsterberg, Hugo, on religiousness of Americans as a people, 319–320.
Murfree, Mary N., 176.

Music, progress of America in, 210–213.
Musical festivals, 212.

N

National Bureau of Education, 223.
Nature, effect of scale on kind of love shown by Americans for, 309–310.
Naval Academy, United States, 223.
Negroes, schools for, 222.
Neighborliness, value placed on, in America, 290–294.
New England, the settlers of, 44–51; fiction dealing with life in, 177; attitude in, toward education, 215; quality of people bred in, 296–297.
New Netherland Company, 53.
Newspapers, American, 28–33; daily story of humanity told in, 184.
New York, Dutch settlement of, 51–55; literature which began in, during provincial period, 119–123; interest in music in, 211–212.
"New York, History of," Irving's, 121–122.
Nitobe, Dr., criticism of Bryant's "To a Waterfowl" by, 301.
Norris, Frank, 181–182.
Novel, the modern American, 172–182.

O

"Old Creole Days," Cable's, 175.
Opportunity, America as the land of, 285.

z 337

INDEX

Orchestras in modern America, 211–212.
Otis, James, 109.

P

Page, Thomas Nelson, 175.
Painting, American, 194–203.
Palmer, work in sculpture by, 208.
Pamphlets of Revolutionary period, 108.
Parish schools of Roman Catholic Church, 222.
Parkman, Francis, 170.
Partridge, William Ordway, 209.
Pasteur, Louis, on democracy, 20.
Peale, American painter, 194, 196.
Pedagogy, education in, 258–259.
Penn, William, 55.
Pennsylvania, settlement of, 55–56.
"Père Goriot," a Parisian rather than French novel, 173.
Perry, Bliss, 186.
Philadelphia, painters of, 196.
Physical training at American colleges, 241–242.
Pilgrims, the, 51.
"Pilot," Cooper's, 146.
Pioneers in Western States, 85–87.
Plymouth, Mass., settlement of, 44.
Poe, Edgar Allan, consideration of work of, 149–152.
Poetry, comparative decline in vogue of, 184; modern exponents of, 185; themes of present-day, 185–186.
Political organization of American nation, 274–275.
Politicians and good-fellowship, 291–292.
Polytechnic Institute, Troy, 258.

Powers, "Greek Slave" of, 204; limitations of, as a sculptor, 206.
Pratt, Bela, 209.
"Precaution," Cooper's, 146.
Prescott, W. H., 169.
Presidents of United States, education and intellectual attainments of, 14–16, 245–246.
Princeton University, 220.
Protection, policy of, contrasted with customary self-reliance of Americans, 284.
Puritanism, rise of, 47–48; characteristics of, 48 ff.; the spirit of freedom in, 50.

Q

Quakers in America, 55–56; John Woolman a notable representative of the, 116–118.
Queen Anne architecture in America, 193, 193.

R

Races, variety of, in composition of Americans, 42–60; intermingling of, in every nation, 267–269.
Radcliffe College, 237.
Railroads, transcontinental, 90.
"Red Rover," Cooper's, 146.
Reform movements in America, 323–325.
Religion, place of, in American civilization, 317 ff.
Republicans, early party of, led by Jefferson, 79.
Research work at universities, 260–261; special foundations for, 262 ff.
Rhodes, James Ford, 172.

INDEX

"Rip Van Winkle," Irving's, 123.
"Rise of Silas Lapham," Howells', 179–180.
Rockefeller Institute for Medical Research, 262–263.
Roosevelt, Theodore, 15–16.
"Rubáiyát," Vedder's illustrations for, 198–199.
Ruckstuhl, "Spirit of the Confederacy" of, 209.
Russell Sage Foundation for investigation and eradication of causes of poverty and ignorance, 265.

S

Sabbath, the American, 318–319.
Saint Gaudens, Augustus, 207.
St. Paul's School, 225.
Sargent, John S., 203.
Scale, impress of, on American literature, thought, and character, 298 ff.
"Scarlet Letter," Hawthorne's, 143–144.
Schools, early American, 214 ff. See Education.
Schouler, James, 172.
"Science of English Verse," Lanier's, 165.
Scientific universities, 257–258.
Scotch-Irish in America, 55, 56, 57, 58.
Sculpture, American, 203–210.
Sedgwick, Henry D., 186.
Shaw Memorial, Boston, 208.
Sherborne house, Portsmouth, 190.
Sherman Memorial, New York, 208.
"Sketch Book," Irving's, 122.

Slavery, introduction of, 43; restiveness of Americans under existence of, and final destruction, 323.
Smith, John, narrative of adventures of, 105.
Smith College, 237.
South, the settlers of the, 42–44, 56–58; fiction writers of the, 174–176; activities of General Education Board concerning the, 263; effect of climate on men and manners in the, 297–298.
Southern Education Board, 264–265.
"Spy, The," Cooper's, 145, 146–147.
"Star-Spangled Banner, The," 155, 210–211.
State government, lines of demarcation between national government and, 75–77, 156.
State universities, 247–248, 251–253; pedagogic training in, 258.
Steamboat, invention of the, 82–83.
Stevens Institute, 258.
Story, William Wetmore, 208–209.
Stowe, Harriet Beecher, 178–179.
Stuart, Gilbert, 194, 196.
Suffrage, American belief in universal, 17.
Supreme Court, functions of the, 275; decision that America is a Christian nation, 320–321.
Swedish blood in America, 56, 58.

T

Taft, Lorado, 210.
Taft, William H., 15.

INDEX

Tariff, the American, 284.
Teachers, pensions for, by Carnegie Foundation, 264.
Teachers College, Columbia University, 258.
Teaching, training in science of, 258-259.
Tennessee mountaineers in fiction, 176.
Thackeray, W. M., on Irving, 123.
"Thanatopsis," Bryant's, 128, 145.
Thoreau, H. D., "Maine Woods" of, contrasted with White's "Natural History of Selbourne," 310.
"To a Waterfowl," Bryant's, 135; reason for tendency to moralization in, 301-302.
"Tom Sawyer," 176.
Trumbull, American painter, 196.
Tuskegee Institute, 283.

U

"Uncle Remus" stories, 176.
"Uncle Tom's Cabin," 178-179.
Universities, American, 219-220, 245 ff.; state, 247-248, 251-253; educational influence from Europe upon American, 254-257; scientific, 257-258; close relation of technical training of all kinds with, 259-260.
University, significance of the word, as applied to American educational institutions, 253-254.

V

Van Dyke, Henry, 185, 186.
"Vanity Fair," not a national novel, 173.
Vassar College, 237.

Vedder, Elihu, 198-199.
Vespucci, Amerigo, 41.
Virginia, the settlers of, 42-44; beginnings of education in, 215-216.
Virginia, University of, 113, 220.
Virginia Company, educational plans of, 215.
"Virginian," Wister's, 181.

W

"War and Peace," as a national novel, 173.
War between the States, misconception of, by foreign nations, 8; birth of the Nation dating from, 153, 158.
Ward, J. Q. A., 207.
Washington, George, 15, 44; the guiding genius of America, 70-71, 73; election to Presidency, 77; bequest by, for founding of a national university, 219-220.
Wealth, vastness of increase of, in America, and effects, 311-314.
Wellesley College, 237.
Wells College, 237.
West, development of the, 83 ff.; fiction dealing with the, 176-177; effect of climate on men and manners in the, 298.
West, Benjamin, 196, 197.
Whistler, J. McN., 200-202.
White, William Allen, 181.
Whitman, Walt, discussion of work of, 160-164.
Whitney, Eli, 83.
Whittier, J. G., 136.
William and Mary College, 218.
Wilson, Woodrow, 15; on keeping the doors of opportunity open to Americans, 289.

INDEX

Wister, Owen, 177, 181.
Women, college education for, 236-238.
Woodberry, G. E., 185.
Woolman, John, 116-118.
Wren, Sir Christopher, inspiration of, in American colonial architecture, 189-190.
Wyant, Alexander H., 198, 199.

Y

Yale College, founding of, 218; spirit actuating athletics at, 241; significance of word "university" as applied to, 253.
Yorktown, epoch-making surrender of British at, 68.